Inspiring Thoughts to

JUMP-START YOUR DAY

Aug 2019

Bro. Wayne Blakely,
Thanks for your service to
our CFC prayerline ministry
thru the years.

[signature]

SIMEON P. ROSETE JR., DBS

PAGE PUBLISHING, INC.
New York, NY

First originally published by Page Publishing, Inc. 2019

ISBN 978-1-64544-047-5 (Paperback)
ISBN 978-1-64544-048-2 (Digital)

Printed in the United States of America

To Ellen Pacheco Rosete, the beautiful love of my life who has been my faithful and steady partner through all the forty-seven years of my ministry, I dedicate this book.

Introduction

THE MATERIALS IN this volume are messages that I placed in the weekly church bulletin as an encouragement to the members of my congregation through the years. In addition to the weekly sermon, I thought it best to give them a short devotional thought that they could take home with them following the church service that they could meditate on the following week and through the rest of their lives.

It is a compilation of my experiences and thoughts while I pastored my flock together with a host of materials that I have gathered from a variety of sources through the years. It didn't take long before I learned how my congregation was being richly blessed by these messages and that they were filing them for future reference. Some of them mentioned how it became a convenient source of short inspirational messages that they themselves delivered when the occasion arose.

Then the idea came from a number of these friends. Why don't I publish them in book form and have it circulated as wide as possible so that many more people could be blessed. That is how this book came into being.

Needless to say, many of the materials have been edited and may appear slightly different from their original format in order to suit the reading public. But a number of them still retain some of the characteristics of a narrative that relates some of the experiences of the life and ministry of the congregation.

In whatever form they show up in this volume, I trust that you will find the materials to be uplifting and truly devotional that will jump-start your day and help make each day of your life worth living.

Acknowledgments

I WANT TO express appreciation to the members of the Central Filipino Church of Seventh-day Adventists at Los Angeles, California, who called me from my ministerial work in the Philippines to come and serve them as their senior pastor. They have been an encouragement and support to my ministry through all the twenty-five years that I have been with them to the present day. It was to them that these messages were initially directed. My thanks go especially to Dr. Alfonso Miguel Jr. and Rey Regoso, head elder and associate head elder respectively.

My gratitude goes to the administrative committee of the Southern California Conference of Seventh-day Adventists for allowing me a three-month sabbatical leave; within that time I was able to put the finishing touches on this book. I thank Velino Salazar, president; James Lee, vice president; John Cress, executive secretary; Orville Ortiz, chief financial officer; and Royal Harrison, Greg Hoenes, Gerard Kiemeney, Luis Pena, and Samuel Lee, region directors.

I like to thank Dianne Fabrigar Cruz for her invaluable assistance in collecting and retrieving these materials from files in years past in our church office with her efficiency and computer skills.

I also want to thank my family for the support they gave to this project. My wife, Ellen, has allowed me the time to write and my children: Joenilyn and husband, Wilfredo Navarro Jr., Jocelyn, Samuel, Jane and husband, Carlo Verde, and my grandkids: Katelynn, Ariana, Ella, and Cruz for being such an inspiration in the production of this material.

CONTENTS

Have a Fun Day!

THE GOOD NEWS for today is that if you are having fun, chances are you will stay healthy. Arthur Stone, a psychologist at State University of New York, has done studies to show that pleasant experiences improve the functioning of the body's immune system for three days—the fun day plus two freebies. A negative experience has the opposite effect, but it lasts only for one day.

So plan your day and be sure to make it a fun day. Having at least two fun days spread three days apart can take care of the body's immune system all week.

Isn't this what the Bible is talking about when it says that "a merry heart does good like a medicine and that a broken spirit dries up the bones"? (Proverbs 17:22).

Then put fun into your day. Plan happy times. Think joyful thoughts. Wear that smile on the face. And enjoy your good health.

Just for Today

OFTENTIMES WE WORRY too much about tomorrow and the days ahead. If our company downsizes, will we be able to keep our jobs, or are we going to be the first to go? When we retire, will there be enough funds left to pay our social security pension? Will our retirement money be sufficient to sustain the lifestyle of our choice? Will our health sustain us and carry us to the ripe old age of the eighties or even nineties? Or will some ailment of a terminal nature sneak up on us, cutting short our earthly pilgrimage?

These and many more unnecessary concerns about the future crowd out our minds to such extent as to rob us of the joys and pleasures of the moment. And to think that tomorrow is not yet and the only thing we have in our hands is today. How about simply thanking God for his precious gift of today and living it up to the fullest in the way he wants us to live.

Someone wrote the following material about what we can do "just for today…"

- Smile at a stranger.
- Listen to someone's heart.
- Drop a coin where a child can find it.
- Learn something new, then teach it to someone else.
- Tell someone you're thinking of them.
- Hug a loved one.
- Don't hold a grudge.
- Don't be afraid to say "I'm sorry."

- Look a child in the eye, and tell them how great they are.
- Don't kill that spider in your house. He's just lost, so show him the way out.
- Look beyond the face of a person into their heart.
- Make a promise and keep it.
- Call someone for no other reason than to just say "hi."
- Show kindness to an animal.
- Stand up for what you believe in.
- Smell the rain, feel the breeze, listen to the wind, enjoy the sun.
- Use all your senses to their fullest.
- Cherish all your *todays*!

Great advice for today, any day, and *every day*.

Jesus said, "But seek first the kingdom of God and His righteousness, and all these things shall be added to you. Therefore do not worry about tomorrow, for tomorrow will worry about its own things. Sufficient for the day is its own trouble" (Matthew 6:33–34).

Slowing Down

EACH NEW DAY is a gift from God. What we do with it is our gift to him. And what better gift can we present than to live a life that honors God and be a blessing to others.

The psalmist prays, "Teach us to number our days that we may apply our hearts unto wisdom" (Psalm 90:12).

We have to admit that the dizzying pace of life is taking away the joy and zest for living. And life in the fast lane has also blurred in our minds the very reason for our existence. Constant exposure to the hustle and bustle and hurry and worry is what is causing so many physical and emotional problems such as angry outbursts, anxiety, depression, fatigue, rashes, insomnia, hair loss, and sharp weight gain or loss.

As we begin each day, I have some suggestions for us to be able to recapture the purpose of living and have a happier, healthier life. Here are the following:

1. Develop a mind-set. Have a philosophy of life. Establish your goals. Set your priorities. Ask yourself the purpose of your life. Then reorder your life to the achievement of that objective.
2. Have a daily quiet time. This could be anytime, but for most, the early morning hours would be best. This could be the most productive time in your day. Use this time to pray to God, commune with your soul, and plan your day. This can even be a buffer zone in the midst of your

appointments to give your brain and body some stress-free breathing space.

3. Balance your activities. If your job is mentally demanding, do something that is physical and vice versa. This gives you more energy and well-being as all your faculties are put to use.

4. Laugh more. Studies show that laughter promotes better blood circulation, stimulates blood pressure, and prompts the brain to release endorphins and other compounds that reduce pain.

5. Be a child again. Children know how to have a good time. They act spontaneously, laugh, are trusting, are not afraid to make mistakes, and accept life as it is.

6. Get away and do nothing. Change locations. See the world. Even an afternoon drive into the country or along the coast can soothe a frenzied mind and troubled spirit.

7. Cultivate the attitude of gratitude. Happy people are thankful people. It is impossible to be uptight, tense, and frenzied when your heart is overflowing with gratitude.

What's Your Life's Purpose?

JOSH MCDOWELL TELLS about an executive "headhunter" who recruits corporate executives for large firms. This headhunter once told McDowell that when he interviews an executive, he likes to disarm him. "I offer him a drink," said the headhunter, "take off my coat, undo my tie, throw up my feet, and talk about baseball, football, family, whatever until he's all relaxed. Then when I think I've got him relaxed, I lean over, look him straight in the eye, and say, 'What's your purpose in life?' It's amazing how top executives fall apart at that question."

Then he told about interviewing one fellow recently. He had him all disarmed, had his feet up on his desk, talking about football. Then the headhunter leaned over and said, "What's your purpose in life, Bob?" And the executive said, without blinking an eye, "To go to heaven and take as many people with me as I can."

"For the first time in my career," said the headhunter, "I was speechless." No wonder. He had encountered someone who was prepared. He was ready.

His purpose—"to go to heaven and take as many people with me as I can."

Life's purpose is what gives meaning in life. It is the destination at the end of the road. It is what makes the journey bearable when the road becomes bumpy and when the sailing gets rough. It is the spring in the gait, the quickening of the pace, the sparkle in the eye, the smile on the lips, and the enthusiasm in the voice. It is the light at the end of the tunnel, and the hope when all around is gloom and doom.

The question for you is, "Do you have a purpose in life? And is your purpose like that of the executive to go to heaven and take as many people with you as you can?"

Living a Balanced Life

IN LIFE, WE experience a variety of contrasts and opposites. There are night and day, hot and cold, high and low, pleasure and pain, joy and sorrow. We may have a preference for one and a discomfort for the other. But just the same, patiently enduring one prepares our hearts and minds to savor the other.

Carl Jung, a Swiss psychiatrist, writes, "There are as many nights as days, and the one is just as long as the other in the year's course. Even a happy life cannot be without a measure of darkness, and the word 'happy' would lose its meaning if it were not balanced by sadness."

In a less-than-perfect world, this is our lot. One day soon, Jesus will come to bring all things to their original perfection. But until then, let us be grateful for everything we experience that helps put balance into our earthly lives.

Advice for a Life of Fulfillment

IF YOU ARE like most people, you may have made resolutions at the beginning of the year. You have set goals you want to achieve and have mapped out strategies that would help you make these dreams come true. I trust that you are doing well in the context of these goals, by the grace of God.

I just want to share with you something that got my attention that can inspire and assist you as you move on in life. It comes in the form of a general advice on how to live a successful and fulfilling life. Consider the following:

1. Don't use time or words carelessly. Neither can be retrieved.
2. Don't be afraid to learn. Knowledge is weightless, a treasure you can carry easily.
3. Don't run through life so fast that you forget not only where you've been but also where you are going.
4. Don't shut love out of your life by saying it's impossible to find. The quickest way to receive love is to give it away; the faster way to lose love is to hold it too tightly; and the best way to keep love is to give it wings.
5. Don't be afraid to encounter risk. It is by taking chances that we learn how to be brave.
6. Don't be afraid to admit you are less than perfect. It is this fragile thread that binds us together.
7. Don't give up when you still have something to give. Nothing is really over until the moment you stop trying.

8. Don't let your life slip through your fingers by living in the past or future. By living your life one day at a time, you live *all* the days of your life.

9. Don't take for granted the closest things to your heart. Cling to them as you would your life, for without them, life is meaningless.

10. Don't set your goals by what other people deem important. Only you know what is best for you.

11. Don't undermine your worth by comparing yourself with others. It is because we are different that each of us is special.

I am very sure that if you heed these instructions, you will find happiness and success in life. So grab life by the horns, and relish each moment that it brings.

Twenty-Five Things Life Has Taught Me

I WOKE UP today with a bad headache- something I haven't had for a long time. I wondered why, though I knew I was somewhat under the weather all week last week, what with the rains and the frigid temperatures. And the long day at church yesterday didn't help much—preaching, chairing committees, teaching Bible classes, and holding a board meeting that lasted well into the night.

But today is my birthday and I am determined to make it a rather special and memorable one. Not wanting to simply lament my situation and to engage in self-pity just because things were not going the way I wanted them to go on my special day, I pulled my tablet from the nightstand and started to gather my thoughts, putting down what sixty-five years of life have taught me.

And here I share them with you. They come in no sequential order of importance. I have them down as they occurred to me while trying to ignore the pain:

1. I learned that some friends may be good for only a season and for a specific purpose; so cherish them while you may.
2. I learned that relatives are a safety net in an unpredictably crazy world.
3. I learned that the world is a mirror that reflects attitudes and promptings of the innermost core of one's being.
4. I learned that grandkids are a comfort to the aches and pains of old age.

5. I learned that service is the rent we pay for the space we occupy on earth.

6. I learned that children serve as the biggest reason that propels us to bigger and better things.

7. I learned that success in life doesn't come in the form of possessions acquired or academic degrees earned; it comes rather in the amount of contributions we have made to make the world a better place.

8. I learned that Christianity is not a religion of do's and don't's. It is simply living the life that Jesus lived.

9. I learned that church is not a place where one comes to listen to wonderful music and great preaching. It is a place where one comes to worship God and gets filled with his presence to a point that he is eager to go out to serve a world that is desperately in need of his witness.

10. I learned that relationships complete and enrich our lives. Take time to grow and nurture them.

11. I learned that humor and laughter bring healing to the soul. And they make the journey seem a lot shorter.

12. I learned that life is what we make it—given the building blocks of our heredity and environment.

13. I learned that happiness is a by-product that comes to us from serving others and doing God's will in our lives, not something that we catch at the end of a long chase.

14. I learned that true wealth is not measured in dollars and cents, or even in the number of cars and other material possessions. It is measured by the degree of contentment we have with the blessings of life and the absence of the desire for evanescent and transitory things.

15. I learned that real poverty comes the moment one surrenders all aspirations and dreams for a better and more meaningful life.

16. I learned that troubles in life push us to limitless heights— in much the same way that the wind catapults a kite to the heavens.

17. I learned that life's blessings are to be enjoyed to show gratitude to God who is the giver and source of every good and perfect gift, and to be shared with others who are desperate for a lift in their journey.
18. I learned that time is what God allows each one to accomplish the task he has for us on earth.
19. I learned that a little more cash gives one the ability to open more doors and go farther in life.
20. I learned that a smile on the face is the most important article in one's makeup kit.
21. I learned that health is a treasure that should be preserved and cherished at all costs. Without it, length of years and abundance of possessions do not count for much.
22. I learned that work is what we have to do to be able to afford the things we like to do. But he who loves his job saves himself lots of money and finds looking for a reason to retire difficult.
23. I learned that retirement is what we get into when we think we will be happier not having a job as opposed to having one.
24. I learned that freedom in the realm of the spirit is not the ability to do anything you want any which way you like but the power to do what needs to be done in the battle for the right.
25. I learned that destiny is where we find ourselves as a result of God's saving grace and the use of our gift of choice.

I praise God for his abundant blessings and for all the joys that have been mine through the years. I look forward to the years ahead as I put my hand in his and trust him to lead all the way.

Carrots, Eggs, and Coffee Beans

A YOUNG WOMAN went to her mother and told her about her life and how things were so hard for her. She did not know how she was going to make it and wanted to give up. She was tired of fighting and struggling. It seemed as one problem was solved, a new one arose.

Her mother took her to the kitchen. She filled three pots with water and placed each one on a high fire. Soon the pots came to a boil. In the first, she placed carrots, in the second, she placed eggs, and in the last, she placed ground coffee beans. She let them sit and boil without saying a word.

In about twenty minutes, she turned off the burners. She fished the carrots out and placed them in a bowl. She pulled the eggs out and placed them in a bowl. Then she ladled the coffee out and placed it in a bowl. Turning to her daughter, she asked, "Tell me what you see."

"Carrots, eggs, and coffee," she replied.

Her mother brought her closer and asked her to feel the carrots. She did and noted that they were soft. The mother then asked the daughter to take an egg and break it. After pulling off the shell, she observed the hard-boiled egg. Finally, the mother asked the daughter to sip the coffee. The daughter smiled as she tasted its rich aroma. The daughter then asked, "What does it mean, Mother?"

Her mother explained that each of the objects had faced the same adversity: boiling water. Each reacted differently. The carrot went in strong, hard, and unrelenting. However, after being subjected to the boiling water, it softened and became weak. The egg had been fragile. Its thin outer shell had protected its liquid interior, but after sitting through the boiling water, its inside became hardened. The ground coffee beans were unique, however. After they were in the boiling water, they had changed the water.

"Which are you?" she asked her daughter. "When adversity knocks on your door, how do you respond? Are you a carrot, an egg, or a coffee bean?"

This is a story with some precious lessons for us to learn about life. As we face trials and challenges, it will be well for us to ask ourselves the question: Which one am I? Am I the carrot that starts strong but softens and wilt during pain and adversity? Am I the egg that starts with a tender and sensitive heart but becomes hardened and stiff when I experience the loss of a loved one, a relationship break-down, or financial hardship? Or am I like the coffee bean, changing the hot water, the very circumstances that brought the pain?

When the water gets hot, do I release my fragrance and flavor? Like the bean, do I get better and try to change the situation around me? When the hour is darkest, and the trials are at their greatest, do I elevate myself to another level?

So again, are you a carrot, an egg, or a coffee bean?

Recharging Your Spiritual Batteries

STRESS IS A part of daily life. In fact, a reasonable amount of it is good if one is to live an exciting and challenging life. This was observed even among monkeys and other smaller animals who were placed in cages that were adjacent to those of lions and tigers when they were shipped from their native Africa to the New World. When they arrived, they were found to be in generally better health than those whose circumstances were not the same.

But too much stress for too long can result in burnout and other physical ailments such as ulcers, strokes, and even heart attacks. So it is important to learn how to live so that you can beat burnout and the other risky health conditions that come with it.

The following suggestions are from the February 2007 issue of the *Reader's Digest* that I took at liberty to comment and expand on.

1. Make time for yourself. God himself rested on the seventh day during the Creation week to give us an example that we need to give our bodies physical, mental, social, and spiritual rest. We need to recharge our batteries, and we need time for this.

2. Develop a method to calm yourself. When tension builds up, take a deep breath, meditate, or better still, pray. When freeway driving in Los Angeles sometimes gets scary, tight, and fast, I tell my wife to just close her eyes. Of course, that means she can pray, but one thing she doesn't have to see is

the blur of traffic whizzing by. Have you seen the bumper sticker, "Pray for me. I drive in LA"?

When doing meetings in the board, sometimes things come to a stalemate, and the atmosphere of the room gets tense. I sometimes try to look at some humorous side of the situation, and when I share my observation, I usually get a laugh. When that happens, everyone loosens up, and we can do business again.

3. Analyze what you love and hate about your job. The goal is to organize your work so that you are focusing more and spending more of your time and energy on the things that you love and less of yourself on the things you hate about your job.

4. Settle for less than perfect. Don't be a perfectionist; otherwise, you will stall, and delaying will stress you as you try to beat deadlines for your work. I have been working on some courses of study, and my desire to be perfect in every area has caused me some problems and stressed me out on the completion dates. When I tried to settle for less, although I gave it my best, I found myself breezing through my work, and I still got the marks I had hoped for.

5. Take good care of yourself. You won't be able to help others unless you took care of yourself first. Airline safety instructions emphasize the importance of putting on your gas mask and life jacket first in the event of an emergency even before attending to the needs of your child. When Jesus commands us to "love your neighbor as you love yourself," he means that we must have a proper love for ourselves first before we can truly love others. We need to have a proper self-esteem and self-worth before we can truly affect others for God.

6. Cultivate a support network. God has never planned for us to live in isolation. He said at the Creation, "It is not good for man to be alone." Of course, this was made in the context of marriage and family, but just the same, we have been created to be social beings—beings in relation. We

need others to be able to grow, enjoy life, and maximize our potential. Paul would later say, "No man liveth to himself." And an English poet would put this truth into the words of an immortal song, "No Man Is an Island; No Man Stands Alone." Let us have a network of support that we can share our joys and triumphs with, people we can fall back and lean on when our world comes crashing down on us.

7. Set limits. Superman exists only on the silver screen. We have to admit we are humans, and as such, we have our own limitations. So know your limits, and when you get somewhere near there, respect your body and put your foot on the brakes.

8. Learn to say "no" in a firm but respectful way. Everybody will be happier in the end.

9. Plan for the future. Have an anticipation of what is coming next. When you know your next move, you have a feeling that you are already a winner. You have a sense of control of your life. You won't be caught flat-footed. You won't be stressed about "What will happen if…"

10. Trust in God. You won't be able to know just exactly what the future holds. And you do not need to know. All that matters is that you know who holds tomorrow. And you need to know that he holds your hands.

Let Go and Let God

THE FOLLOWING MATERIAL could have been taken straight from the Bible. It is based on scriptural principles and couched in a language and phraseology those of us in the day-to-day business of living are familiar with.

It's pretty much like Jesus saying, "Don't worry... Isn't life more than food and the body more than clothing?" (Matthew 6:25).

There are other more important things that you should be thinking about. And if you have those, there is no reason for you to be unhappy or dissatisfied with the way things are going in your life right now.

Consider the following material as a direct communiqué from God who is in charge of life in this universe.

Memo from God

Today I will be handling all of your problems. Remember that I do not need your help. If life happens to deliver a situation to you that you cannot handle, do not attempt to resolve it. Put it in the SFGTD (Something For God To Do) box. And remember that all situations will be resolved in my time, not yours.

Once the matter is placed in the box, do not hold onto it by worrying about it. Instead, focus on all the wonderful things that are present in your life right now.

If you find yourself stuck in traffic, don't despair. There are people in this world for whom driving is an unheard of privilege.

Should you have a bad day at work, think of the man who has been out of work for years.

Should you despair over a relationship gone bad, think of the person who has never known what it's like to love and be loved in return.

Should you grieve the passing of another weekend, think of the woman in dire straits, working twelve hours a day, seven days a week to feed her children.

Should your car break down, leaving you miles away from assistance, think of the paraplegic who would love the opportunity to take that walk.

Should you notice a new gray hair in the mirror, think of the cancer patient in chemotherapy who wishes she had hair.

Should you find yourself at a loss and pondering what life is all about, asking what your purpose in life is, be thankful. There are those who did not live long enough to get that opportunity.

Should you find yourself the victim of other people's bitterness, ignorance, smallness, or insecurities, remember, things could be worse. You could be one of them.

And again, it's all about letting go and letting God.

ASAP

HAVE YOU EVER received letters or invitations asking you to respond or do something with the letters ASAP coming after them? Of course, it means "As Soon As Possible." This abbreviation also tells us of the hurry, worry, and stress that are so much a part of our day-to-day lives.

If we think of it in a different manner, however, we may begin to find a new way of dealing with the rough times of our lives. And what it should really stand for is Always Say A Prayer. In fact, there is a poem by Lisa Engelhardt that deals with this thought, and I could not have said it any better than she has put in this poem.

Always Say A Prayer

There's work to do, deadlines to meet
You have no time to spare.
But as you hurry and scurry...
Always Say A Prayer.

In the midst of family chaos,
"Quality time" is rare.
Do your best; let God do the rest
Always Say A Prayer.

It may seem like your worries
Are more than you can bear.

SIMEON P. ROSETE JR., DBS

Slow down and take a breather
Always Say A Prayer.

God knows how stressful life can be,
And He wants to ease your cares.
He'll respond to all your needs...
Always Say A Prayer.

The apostle Peter speaks this truth essentially when he says in his epistle, "Casting all your cares upon Him for He cares for you" (1 Peter 5:7).

Fourteen Ingredients of Love

IN 1 CORINTHIANS 13:4–8 (NIV), we read the following, "Love is patient, love is kind. It does not envy, it does not boast, it is not proud. It is not rude, it is not self-seeking, it is not easily angered, it keeps no record of wrongs. Love does not delight in evil but rejoices with the truth. It always protects, always trusts, always hopes, always perseveres. All the special gifts and powers from God will someday come to an end, but love goes on forever."

This is what true love is all about. It is the kind that originates from above. As we can see, it has fourteen ingredients. Paul spells out clearly for us just what they are:

1. Love is patient. Literally, love suffers long; it has a long fuse. When Jesus was wronged, he was patient and silent.
2. Love is kind. Love is going out of our way to be full of grace toward others.
3. Love does not envy. Unconditional love desires the best for others. Our main goal is for our beloved to be all God intends them to be.
4. Love does not boast. The Greek here implies we do not boast like a "wind bag." Jesus never showed off. His greatness is often revealed in what he suppressed rather than what he did or said.
5. Love is not proud. God's love is not arrogant. Pride is inflated selfishness. Love is genuine humility.
6. Love is not rude. It is never inconsiderate or inattentive.

7. Love is not self-seeking. God's love does not grasp for its own rights. This rules out selfish, conditional types of love—the I-love-you-if- and the I-love-you-because loves.
8. Love is not easily angered. It does not become irritated. It is not touchy. Jesus was never vindictive. He never retaliated when wronged. He never grumbled or had a bad temper. (His temple cleansing was a controlled and calculated response.)
9. Love keeps no record of wrongs. God's love forgives and forgets. Jesus came to blot out our sins and remember them no more.
10. Love does not delight in evil, but it rejoices in truth. Love is never glad when others do wrong or wrongs happen to others. It does not delight in the weakness of others. It does not gloat or gossip.
11. Love always trusts and believes all things. God's love gives the benefit of the doubt. It is loyal, yet not gullible. It is tolerant in judging others.
12. Love always hopes. It never takes failure as final. It always looks toward the future, not the past.
13. Love always perseveres. It endures all. God's love cannot be conquered. If we endure with Christ, we will reign with Him.
14. Love goes on forever. Love is eternal. It never fails. It never loses strength. It never leaves its place. It is immovable and indefatigable.

So there you have them, the fourteen ingredients of love. But I want you to do something else. I want you to read the list and replace the word "love" with "Jesus." It fits, doesn't it? God is love.

And so we know and rely on the love God has for us. God is love. Whoever lives in love lives in God, and God in Him (1 John 4:16, NIV).

It's Your Choice

EVERY DAY WE are faced with choices. And we have to make them. Even not choosing to make them is a choice. But it is important what we choose because that is what it's going to be for us. Someone said it well when he said, "Life is what we make it." There may be two people indoors on a rainy day. One may be feeling so miserable while another may be having the time of his life. Two people, same day, yet there are two different reactions. It's all in how we look at it.

An anonymous author penned the following words:

> Today I can complain because the weather is rainy or I can be thankful that the grass is getting watered for free.
> Today I can feel sad that I don't have more money or I can be glad that my finances encourage me to plan my purchases wisely and guide me away from waste.
> Today I can grumble about my health or I can rejoice that I am alive.
> Today I can cry because roses have thorns or I can celebrate that thorns have roses.
> Today I can mourn my lack of friends or can excitedly embark upon a quest to discover new relationships.

Today I can whine because I have to go to work
    or I can shout for joy because I have a job
    to do.
Today stretches ahead of me, waiting to be
    shaped. And here I am, the sculptor who
    gets to do the shaping. What today will be
    like, is up to me.
I get to choose what kind of day I will have.

So you make the choice. And choose well because I guarantee that's exactly what today will be like.

But best of all, choose Jesus—because when you do, you have everything. And everything will go well with you. Choose well, therefore, today and every day of your life.

The Golden Rules of Successful Living

IN THE JANUARY 2012 issue of *Reader's Digest*, the editors suggest four golden rules to follow to help us follow through with the resolutions we make from time to time. They are the following:

1. Measure up. This means to know your cholesterol and blood pressure numbers and to make sure you set up appointments for all the health screenings you should get.
2. Move more. Do more exercise and get at least thirty minutes of it every day.
3. Eat well. Choose your food well and make healthy eating decisions.
4. Enjoy life. Relieve yourself of stress and live happier.

I like to emphasize on the last one because we take it for granted, and yet it is a major factor in successful living. The big secret here is to do more of what you enjoy. Having meaningful relationships and maintaining a positive outlook give one's health a huge boost, not just mentally but physically as well.

So an important key to successful living is to love more, laugh more, and enjoy more. And you'll find that life is worth living when you do things that are important and meaningful in your life.

Wasn't this what Paul was telling the Philippians 4:4? "Rejoice in the Lord always. Again I will say, rejoice!"

Two Forgettable Days

THERE ARE TWO days in every week that we should not worry about. One of these days is yesterday—with its mistakes, shortcomings, and faults. It is past, and there is nothing we can do to bring it back. Whatever happened yesterday, we cannot change it. What is done is done. It is forever beyond our control.

The other day we should not worry about is tomorrow—with its promises, prospects, and possibilities. But tomorrow is not yet here, and we'll never know what it will eventually bring forth.

This leaves us just one day—and that is today. This is actually all we have, and virtually all we need, to live full and significant lives. It is the remorse and bitterness that come as a result of dwelling on the failures of yesterday and the needless anxiety and worry about what may happen tomorrow that rob us of the joy and excitement of living in the beauty of the present that is today.

So forget about yesterday's failures and do not borrow from tomorrow's troubles. Ask God to help you live one day at a time for as Jesus says, "Sufficient for the day is its own trouble" (Matthew 6:34).

The Upward Look

EVERY DAY, AS we journey through life, we meet all kinds of situations. There will be bumps on the road that will jolt us and awaken us to life's harsh realities. We may have to take detours that will slow us down and hamper our progress. Storm clouds may gather and threaten our safety.

But if our eyes are focused on our destination, and we know who walks along with us, holding us by the hand, and watching our every step, we will successfully go through.

There is a poem that speaks to this truth:

> When you are scared or confused,
> And you don't know what to do;
> And you don't know where to turn,
> Always remember this—
>
> Sorrow looks back
> Worry looks around,
> Faith looks up.

The upward look is the look of faith. And it is a look of victory. Because when we look up, we see Jesus the Author and the Finisher of our faith.

Garden of the Heart

SPRING AND SUMMER are my favorite seasons of the year. The whole earth comes to life, and all nature seems to rejoice. This is also the time when I can plant a garden. And I love it because I like to tend and watch things grow. Of course, watching a garden grow is not as much fun as gathering the produce and preparing it for the dinner table. Maintaining a garden is like having a refrigerator. You can always go to it anytime you want fresh vegetables minus the chemicals and other preservatives farmers use to guarantee their freshness.

In my backyard garden, I have a little bit of all my favorite vegetables. There's eggplant, tomato, banana, and bell pepper, bitter melon (ampalaya), spinach, camote, alugbati, string beans, chayote, and a few other herbs. I love watching them grow as they respond to my efforts of aerating the soil, watering, and providing plant food for them.

But there's another garden that I have, and there are some specialty vegetables I like to grow in it. They are squash, turnips, and lettuce. This garden is called "A Church Garden," and I really like to have the following grow on it:

Three Rows of Squash
1. Squash indifference.
2. Squash criticism.
3. Squash gossip.

Four Rows of Turnips
1. Turn up for meetings.
2. Turn up with a smile.
3. Turn up with a visitor.
4. Turn up with a Bible.

Five Rows of Lettuce
1. Let us love one another.
2. Let us welcome strangers.
3. Let us be faithful in duty.
4. Let us truly worship God.
5. Let us give liberally.

Won't you help me plant this kind of garden?

Which Would You Rather Change?

A MAN IN the Army of Alexander the Great, who was also named Alexander, was accused of cowardly actions. He was brought before Alexander who asked what his name was. He replied softly, "Alexander."

"I can't hear you," the ruler stated.

The man again said, a little louder, "Alexander."

The process was repeated one more time, after which Alexander the Great commented, "Either change your name or change your conduct."

The Bible says that Christ's disciples were called "Christians" first in Antioch (near the modern city of Antakya, Turkey) (Acts 11:26). They were called by that name because everything they talked about was Christ, and everything they did was based on the teachings of Christ. The people around them couldn't mistake them for any other group of people. They have to be called Christians because they breathed Christ, sang Christ, talked Christ, and lived like Christ.

No wonder that Paul could say of them, "You are our epistles written in our hearts, known and read of all men" (2 Corinthians 3:2). Like the Christians of old, those of us who live in these last days are to declare in our lives the saving gospel of the Lord Jesus Christ. This is serious, considering that we may be the only Bible that other people see, and the consequences are for all eternity.

So how is our life? Is it more like Christ's, or is it more like the world? Let it reflect the character of Christ more than it reflect the world. Otherwise, it's time we decided to change our conduct or change our name.

Conforming to His Image

In *DISCIPLESHIP JOURNAL*, Carole Mayhall tells of a woman who went to a diet center to lose weight. The director took her to a full-length mirror. On it he outlined a figure and told her, "This is what I want you to be like at the end of the program." Days of intense dieting and exercise followed, and every week, the woman would stand in front of the mirror, discouraged because her bulging outline didn't fit the director's ideal. But she kept at it, and finally one day, she conformed to the longed-for image.

In 2 Corinthians 3:18, Paul writes, "But we all, with open face beholding as in a glass the glory of the Lord, are changed into the same image from glory to glory, [even] as by the Spirit of the Lord."

The goal of every believer is to be transformed into the image of the Lord Jesus Christ. And Paul says the way to do this is to look to Jesus and behold him in his fullness. By constantly beholding him, we become changed into his image from glory unto glory. The mirror from which we can see Christ's image is the mirror of the scriptures. So as we read God's Word every day, we discover the character of Christ, and through the Holy Spirit, we become conformed to His image.

Like the woman in our story, our bulging outline may not fit the image of Christ we see in the scriptures. But if we don't get discouraged, we will eventually be like him through constant prayer, meditation, intense devotion, persistence, and the power of the Holy Spirit.

Consistency and Imagination

OSCAR WILDE SAID, "Consistency is the last refuge of the unimaginative." So stop getting up at 6:00 a.m. Get up at 5:00 a.m. instead. Walk a mile at dawn. Find a new way to drive to work. Switch chores with your spouse next Sunday. Study wildflowers. Plant an herb garden. Read to the blind. Subscribe to an out-of-town paper. Learn a new sport. Canoe at midnight. Travel to places you have never been to before. Learn to speak Spanish (French or Italian). Teach some kid the thing you do best. Listen to two hours of uninterrupted Mozart. Leap out of that rut. Write the story of your life. Savor life. Remember, we pass this way only once.

Consistency is good. And it is important to be consistent in the area of good habits and behavior. But we have to be careful because doing things in the same way day in and day out could lead to boredom and burnout. So even in the doing of good things, we need to be imaginative and creative. Finding new ways to do things can put excitement in our day and add zest and joy in life.

This was King Solomon's message in his book, Ecclesiastes 11:9 when he said:

> Rejoice, O young man, in thy youth; and let thy heart cheer thee in the days of thy youth, and walk in the ways of thine heart, and in the sight of thine eyes: but know thou, that for all these things God will bring thee into judgment.

We should rejoice and enjoy life. Life on earth is too short to be spent in gloom and sadness, bickering and fighting. We need to savor it to its very dregs. However, we need to be ever aware that our actions, words, and thoughts would one day stare us back in the day of judgment.

The Game of Life

BRYAN DYSON, FORMER CEO of Coca-Cola, once gave a thirty-second speech wherein he suggests imagining life as a game in which one is juggling five balls in the air. These are *work*, *family*, *health*, *friends*, and the *spiritual life*. The object of the game is to keep all five in the air.

He further states that it won't be long before one comes to understand that work is a rubber ball. If it drops on the ground, it bounces back. But the other four balls—family, health, friends, and the spiritual life—are made of glass. If one drops them, they will be irrevocably scuffed, marked, nicked, damaged, or even shattered. They will never be the same. And one must come to understand this.

In other words, life is a balancing act. To have a successful and happy life, one must be able to learn how to do well in this balancing act. And while you give time to the important things in life like education, work, and career, make sure you give the more important things the amount of time and attention they deserve.

Successful living is also prioritization. It is putting first things first. Jesus says in Matthew 6:33, "But seek ye first the kingdom of God and His righteousness and all these things shall be added unto you."

Choosing Life's Positives

IN A FALLEN world that we live in, there are two sides to everything. And often these are in striking contrast and disparity with each other. So we have "up and down," "bitter and sweet," "smooth and rough," "happy and sad," "darkness and light," "good and evil," "life and death."

Happiness comes as a result of focusing on the sunnier, brighter side of life. It happens when you take something negative and turn it into a positive experience. Just being positive sets you forth in a nice and beautiful journey. The following positive thoughts that I came across recently are helpful:

1. Don't sleep too much. Enjoy being alive and productive. There'll be plenty of time for that at the end of this life, and Jesus delays his coming.
2. Sometimes, nobody really cares if you are miserable. So you might as well be happy.
3. If you can't find a solution, it is not a problem. It is a reality, and you might as well accept it for you will live with it the rest of your days.
4. Happiness is like perfume. As you pour it on others, you get a few drops on yourself.
5. If in this life all good things must come to an end, then there is good news—all bad things would eventually end too.

The Lord told his people, "I have set before you life and death, blessing and cursing; therefore choose life that both you and your descendants may live" (Deuteronomy 30:19).

Let us choose the positive, and the negatives that come our way, let us turn them into positives. Let us choose life and let the blessings fall. When we choose life, we and our descendants may live.

The Fragile Nature and Uncertainty of Life

WHEN MY WIFE and I and her sister and niece from Toronto, Canada, planned a joint vacation in the Philippines, it was for the purpose of spending some time with an aging mother-in-law and to help her celebrate her birthday—she was going to turn eighty.

But what was expected to be days of fun and laughter turned out to be a time of mourning. And what was planned to be an advance birthday celebration turned out to be a funeral, which reminds us of the uncertainty and fragile nature of life.

But we thank God for allowing her to live a long and fruitful life—a life that was lived to the glory of God and the blessing of fellow men. Neighbors spoke kindly and fondly of her and remembered her many loving deeds. One recipient of her kindness referred to her home as the DSW (department of social welfare) center of the community.

The apostle John in writing the book of Revelation says, "Blessed are those that die in the Lord; yea says the Spirit. For they rest from their labors and their good works do follow them" (14:13).

And we look to that day when Jesus shall come and all the angels with Him. The dead in Christ will be raised back to life, and we shall join them again "in the land of fadeless day."

God Has Been Good

I HAVE BEEN gone for two weeks as I took a group of thirty-five, several of which are from our church, on a journey to the Holy Land. It has been an exciting and memorable trip as we traversed four continents (America, Europe, Africa, and Asia) in a matter of two weeks.

There was a time we walked through three countries in a couple of hours as we crossed the borders of Egypt and Israel and then on through Jordan with the mountains of Saudi Arabia in the distance.

We enjoyed the amazing sights of the Pyramids and the Sphinx along the River Nile. No, we didn't go to the top of Mt. Sinai this time, but we had a chance to see the Well of Moses and the place of the burning bush. Jordan was impressive with the awesome Red Rock City of Petra. But Mt. Nebo was special as we stood where Moses must have stood on top of Mt. Pisgah and could only view the promised land because he could not enter it then.

And of course, the highlight has got to be Israel, the land where Jesus lived. Singing "O Little Town of Bethlehem" at the very place where he was born, sailing on the Sea of Galilee, and visiting the surrounding villages where he spent much of his ministry and performed many of his miracles, spending time at the Garden of Gethsemane where He struggled with the weight of the sins of the world upon his shoulders, walking the via dolorosa and on to Calvary and finally having a communion service at the Garden Tomb in celebration of his resurrection and in anticipation of his soon return.

Through all our journeys, the Lord has preserved and protected us. And we give him the glory and thanks for an experience of a lifetime—making the Bible come alive and renewing our faith in a person who is alive, who is interceding for us in the heavenly courts and one day coming soon to take us home.

I Will Be Here for You

A POEM WRITTEN by Angie Flores basically describes what true friends are and how this gift from God can really be a blessing when we try to be the best of friends to the people whom God has placed on our path. It is full of promises that when fulfilled become blessings to others and in turn become blessings to us as well.

> When you're sad and depressed,
> I will be here to put a smile on your face.
> When you're angry and frustrated,
> I will be here to calm you down.
> When you're hurt and in tears,
> I will be here to wipe them away and mend the
>   pain.
> When you're lonely and have no one,
> I will be here to comfort you.
> When you're feeling unloved and unwanted,
> I will be here to tell you how very important you
>   are.
> When you're having a bad day and need to lash
>   out,
> I will be here to let you let off steam, you can yell
>   at me.
> When there is something on your mind that you
>   need to say,
> I will be here to listen and understand.

When you're lost in confusion,
I will be here to help you figure things out.
When you feel like you're going crazy,
I will be here to bring you back to sanity.
When you are so overwhelmed and need to get
    away,
I will be here with open arms so we can run away
    together.
When you're scared and frightened,
I will be here to protect you and make you feel
    safe.
When you are full of worries,
I will be here to worry with you.
I promise that I will always be here today, tomor-
    row and forever!

Jesus is our greatest friend, and he can do all of these and much more for us. When we act in this manner to our friends, we are allowing our best friend Jesus to shine through and brighten the world around us for his glory. He also said for us to "love one another even as he has loved us" for it is by this sign that the world may know that we are his disciples (John 13:35).

Making and Keeping Friends

WE LIVE IN a society that is so complex that survival is getting more and more difficult. The intense competition in the workplace coupled with our desire to succeed and our own and our families' demands for the finer things of life are taking a toll on the enjoyment of real living.

Perhaps next to faith in God and support from the family, the most important strength we can have is the inspiration and encouragement we get from friends. No matter what happens to our business ventures or our careers, if we have all of the above, we can be sure that life can go on. We can bounce back, and we might even find ourselves on a higher scale of life than where we were at the start.

What follows are some tips on how we can get along with people and can in fact help us win friends and keep them for good:

1. Keep chains on your tongue and always say less than you think. Cultivate a pleasant, persuasive voice. How you say it often counts more than what you say.
2. Make promises sparingly and keep them faithfully.
3. Never let an opportunity pass to say a kind word to somebody. Praise good work, regardless of who did it. If correction is needed, criticize helpfully, never in a destructive manner.
4. Be genuinely interested in others. Let everyone you meet feel that you regard him or her as a person of importance.

5. Be cheerful. Keep the comers of your mouth turned up. Hide your pains, worries, and disappointments under a smile.

6. Keep an open mind on all controversial questions. Discuss without arguing. It is possible to disagree and yet be friendly.

7. Never engage in gossip. Make it a rule to say nothing about another unless it is something good.

8. Be careful of other people's feelings. Laughing at another's expense is rarely worth the effort, and it may hurt when least expected.

9. Pay no attention to cutting remarks that others may make about you. Learn to live above such comments.

10. Don't be too anxious about your rights and having favors repaid. Let the satisfaction of helping others serve as its own reward.

Building Churches in Foreign Lands

In August of 2002, I helped organize a team to partner with Maranatha Builders International on a church-building mission trip to Costa Rica. There were over thirty of us, and membership of the group were mainly from the Los Angeles Central Filipino Church, Glendale Filipino Church, and a few others from Michigan and Florida. Since the work would entail laying bricks and other construction tasks requiring muscles, we made it a point to have a number of young people as part of the group.

As is the case with these projects, we left Costa Rica with a beautifully constructed church for the local believers there after a week of intensive labor. We even had time to go on a sightseeing trip to the natural attractions and tourist sites in the country.

In addition to the joy of having helped provide a place of worship for the believers in the area, the privilege of being able to see the beautiful scenic spots of the land and developing a special bond of friendship and intimacy among members of the group, we also had the wonderful opportunity of experiencing another culture and realizing that the many conveniences and comforts of life we take for granted in the United States are things that can only be dreamed of in other places.

When a similar opportunity of a church-building mission trip to Peru presented itself, I hesitated. This was only because I cherished the marvelous experience we had in our trip to Costa Rica, and I was afraid nothing could ever top it. I wanted to keep that memory protected and untarnished in my mind.

Somehow, in the end I relented, and I got another group going to Peru to build another house of worship for the people in a place called Pucallpa.

The trip was not without difficulties. In addition to the daunting task of completing the church building in six days, we had to contend with the heat and the humidity. (It's summertime in December in Peru.) We had to deal with mosquitoes, bugs, and other insects that are part of jungle life. There was the dust when the sun was out and mud when the rains poured. There was the threat of malaria, typhoid, and yellow fever.

But in everything, God helped us through. Yes, we were generously rewarded with the chance of visiting the amazingly spectacular world-class attraction that is Machu Picchu and experiencing worship at our newly built floating church in the floating islands of Puno in Lake Titicaca, the lake with the highest elevation in the world.

But our sweetest memories are easily the temple of love that has been built in the hearts and minds of our people there whom we have touched and who in turn have touched us and have impacted our lives for time and for eternity.

As a matter of fact, we want to go back—if only to renew our ties with them. But then, other places in the mission field beckon.

Lessons on Life

THERE WAS A man who had four sons. He wanted his sons to learn not to judge things too quickly. So he sent them each on a quest, in turn, to go and look at a pear tree that was a great distance away.

The first son went in the winter, the second in the spring, the third in summer, and the youngest son in the fall.

When they had all gone and come back, he called them together to describe what they had seen.

The first son said that the tree was ugly, bent, and twisted.

The second son said, no, it was covered with green buds and full of promise. The third son disagreed. He said it was laden with blossoms that smelled so sweet and looked so beautiful; it was the most graceful thing he had ever seen.

The last son disagreed with all of them; he said it was ripe and drooping with fruit, full of life, and fulfillment.

The man then explained to his sons that they were all right because they had each seen but only one season in the tree's life.

He told them that one cannot judge a tree, or a person, by only one season and that the essence of who they are and the pleasure, joy, and love that come from that life can only be measured at the end when all the seasons are up.

If you give up when it's winter, you will miss the promise of your spring, the beauty of your summer, and the fulfillment of your fall.

So look at life in perspective. Remember that it is a combination of challenge and fulfillment, of beauty, and promise. Don't let the pain of one season destroy the joy of all the rest. And don't judge life by one difficult season. Persevere through the difficult patches and better times are sure to come sometime later.

Then you can live life to the fullest, taking in the bitter with the sweet, the humdrum with the exciting, the sometimes dull and boring times with the exciting and the spectacular.

Grow or Die

IN THE MARCH 2015 issue of *Reader's Digest*, a quote from Muhammad Ali is included in the Quotable Quotes section. It reads thus:

> The man who views the world at 50 the same as
> he did at 20 has wasted 30 years of his life.

As secular as this man of boxing fame is he is spiritual enough to realize that life on earth is precious. It is dynamic, and it must grow; otherwise, it will simply deteriorate and die. Physically, one may still be alive, but spiritually, he may already be wasted or dead.

The scriptures urge us to grow in our spiritual lives. Or we will be like the schoolroom teacher who when applying for a supervisory position said he had twenty-year experience as an educator.

Knowing about his teaching skills and professional abilities, the interviewer asked, "Do you mean twenty-year experience or one-year experience repeated twenty times?"

That is why we need to grow and not waste our lives. Every day that we live should change us for the better in praising God and giving glory to his name.

The apostle Peter says in his second epistle (chapter 3 verse 18), "But grow in grace and in the knowledge of our Lord and Savior Jesus Christ."

The Gift of Today

EACH DAY COMES to us as a gift from God. Whatever we do with it is entirely up to us. The way we can enjoy it is to use it to honor him and bless others. We can't waste its golden moments lamenting yesterday's mistakes and worrying about tomorrow's events.

And it is important that we use it well because this is the only way it is possible for us to relish memories of the past and look with confidence and anticipation to tomorrow.

Catherine Pulsifer wrote a poem encouraging us to live each day to the fullest and make it the centerpiece of our day-to-day celebration of happy yesterdays and bright tomorrows. We just have to make the choice and act on it.

Today You Can

Today you can choose to count your blessings
    or you can count your troubles.
Today you can live each moment
    or you can put in time.

Today you can take action towards your goals
    or you can procrastinate.
Today you can plan for the future
    or you can regret the past.

Today you can learn one new thing
    or you can stay the same.
Today you can seek possibilities
        or you can overwhelm yourself with the
        impossible.

Today you can continue to move forward
    or you can quit.
Today you can take steps towards resolving your challenges
    or you can procrastinate.

You see today the choices are up to you in deciding
    what you do today.

And Jesus said, "Do not worry about tomorrow, for tomorrow will worry about its own things" (Matthew 6:34).

Live today. Forget about yesterday, and let tomorrow take care of itself.

Top Ten Brain-Damaging Habits

THE SCRIPTURES SAY that we should prosper in all things and be in health even as our soul prospers (3 John 2). And this is because our bodies belong to God and are a dwelling place or temples of the Holy Spirit (1 Corinthians 3:16–17).

Having noted the above principles from God's Word, we should do everything we can to keep healthy and make sure that we are able to serve the Lord in the best way possible. We ought to take good care of our vital organs, especially the brain because this serves as the antenna of the human body to receive and transmit messages to and from heaven.

There are ways to nourish and strengthen the brain. And there are simple things we can avoid in our day-to-day life and environment to help the brain function at its best.

According to the World Health Organization, the top ten biggest brain-damaging habits are the following:

1. No breakfast
2. Overeating
3. Smoking
4. High sugar consumption
5. Air pollution
6. Sleep deprivation
7. Head covered while sleeping
8. Working your brain during illness

9. Lacking in stimulating thoughts
10. Talking rarely

Let us strive to do the best we can so that we can be fit vessels for the Holy Spirit to dwell in and effective instruments for the cause of the kingdom.

You Can Be Whatever You Want to Be

THERE IS A poem attributed to Donna Levine that is very inspirational in the sense that we all can achieve whatever dreams we have if we have the right attitude and the ability to persist in what we purpose to do.

But of course, this can only happen if we team up with the Lord Jesus for through his strength we are able to accomplish things—those that are to his glory and for the blessing of fellowman. Philippians 4:13 says, "I can do all things through Christ who strengthens me."

And Jesus himself reminds us that it is through his power that we can do things because without him, "ye can do nothing" (John 15:5).

> There is inside you
> all of the potential
> to be whatever you want to be,
> all of the energy
> to do whatever you want to do.
>
> Imagine yourself as you would like to be,
> doing what you want to do,
> and each day, take one step
> towards your dream.
>
> And though at times it may seem too
> difficult to continue,
> hold on to your dream.

One morning you will awake to find
that you are the person you dreamed of,
doing what you wanted to do,
simply because you had the courage
to believe in your potential
and to hold on to your dream.

You can do it. As long as you do it with him.

Greater Is He...

WEDNESDAY, JANUARY 13, 2016, is a day that my wife and I would not soon forget. We were driving on the Seventy-One Freeway north at Chino, California, having come from San Diego where we visited Ella, our grandkid, who had surgery that morning.

It was getting dark, about 5:30 p.m., and we were heading straight to church for the midweek prayer meeting. Then all of a sudden, following a brief lapse of concentration on my part, I saw this car in front that had slowed down. I stepped on the brakes, but it was too late. Our car stopped at the moment of impact. Both front airbags deployed, and smoke filled the cabin.

The collision momentarily kept us shocked and frozen on our seats. But we thank the occupants of the other car for their presence of mind, kindness, and helpfulness. They were a young Filipino couple who were nurses, obviously heading home from work. Choosing not to be mad for a potentially serious injury to themselves and heavy damage to their car, they came opening up our car doors, assisting us out of the car, and inquiring if we were okay—showing that sense of care and concern in a moment of crisis.

Looking back two weeks later, we are extremely grateful to God for his protecting care. We feel some aches and pains in various parts of our body, but thank God we've got no broken bones. It could have been worse. Just the other day, there was a footage on TV of a crash of an SUV where the vehicle exploded on impact and caught fire, its two occupants burned to death beyond recognition.

Both our car and the one we rear-ended would be declared a total loss. But that's okay. A car is just a car. At least we are in one piece.

The year was just beginning, and we already had this kind of experience. We don't know what lies ahead, but this we know: God is still in control. And we know he will continue to keep his children safe in the palm of his hands.

I love what the apostle John says, "Greater is He that is in you than he that is in the world" (1 John 4:4).

Eyes on the Goal

As WE MAKE our journey through life, we may already begin to experience obstacles and challenges that cause delays that hamper our progress. While these may distract our attention, they should not in any way obscure our vision of the glorious destination and the worthwhile goals we have set out to achieve.

There could be a lot of excuses that we can use to explain why we are dropping out of the race or are giving up on certain things we have resolved to do. We don't have the resources or wherewithal to continue. We have not adequately prepared for it. We don't have sufficient financial ability. There's not enough support and cooperation from our network of supporters. The goal we have set is not worth the effort and sacrifice we are putting in anyway. And so on, and so forth.

Think about it this way. Imagine a ship that is plowing across the ocean. There's so much water around, and yet the entire water of the sea cannot sink the ship unless it gets inside it. And the ship uses the water to help propel itself toward its desired haven.

In a similar way, negative circumstances and thoughts and all the negativity in the world can't put us down unless we allow them to get inside of us. And we can use them as stepping-stones to greater heights of success and achievement.

And finally, let us heed the words of the apostle Paul who said, "I can do all things through Christ who strengthens me" (Philippians 4:13).

Celebrating Life

IN RECENT WEEKS, death has visited our community and robbed us several of our loved ones. We grieved at our loss and found comfort in the blessed hope of Christ's soon return that will signal the time when we shall be reunited with them.

But these occasions also provided us with time to ponder on life's meaning and to think about ways on how we can live life to its fullest.

There is a material I came across that reminds us about what happens at death and how we should enjoy the gift of life. Consider the following:

> As soon as you die, your identity becomes a "body."
> People use phrases like "bring the body," "lower the body in the grave," "take the body to the graveyard," etc.
> People whom you tried to impress your whole life don't even call you by your name.
> So live a life to impress the Creator, not the creation.
> Take chances.
> Spend money on the things you love.
> Laugh till your stomach hurts.
> Dance even if you are bad at it.
> Pose stupidly for photos.
> Be like a child again.

> After all, death is not the greatest loss in life. The
> greatest loss is when life dies inside you while
> you are alive.
> Celebrate this event called life.

The wise man admonishes, "Whatever your hand finds to do, do it with your might; for there is no work, nor device, nor knowledge, nor wisdom, in the grave, where you are going" (Ecclesiastes 9:10).

So let us do what we need to do with all the strength and power that we have. For beyond this earthly life that we have is the grave where nothing happens except total cessation of life while we await the resurrection of the just.

Do Not Ask for a Problem-Free Life

WE OFTEN SET goals and commit to certain ideals that we wish to achieve in our lives. But as is the case with so many among us, our energies and determination taper off, and before we realize it, all our vision of an exciting, revitalized, and fun-filled life has vanished into thin air.

The reason this happens is because we shy away from the challenges that come and get overwhelmed by the obstacles and barriers that get thrown our way. We need to have a warrior mentality and fight our way through, never allowing the thought of giving up cross our mind even for once. And as we struggle to make passage through life's difficult twists and turns, we find ourselves getting stronger and building more muscle to be better prepared for the next fray.

As an inspiration to us all, think of the following lines:

> Smooth roads never make good drivers.
> Smooth seas never make good sailors.
> Clear skies never make good pilots.
> Problem-free life never makes a strong and good person!

The apostle James says, "Consider it pure joy, my brothers whenever you face trials of many kinds, because you know that the testing of your faith develops perseverance. Perseverance must finish its work so that you may be mature and complete, not lacking anything" (James 1:2–4).

Adult Lessons from Kids

AT ONE TIME, the disciples asked Jesus who the greatest in the kingdom of heaven was. In reply, Jesus called a little child to him and said, "Unless you are converted and become as little children, you will by no means enter the kingdom of heaven. Therefore, whoever humbles himself as this little child is the greatest in the kingdom of heaven" (Matthew 18:1–4).

Commenting on these scriptures, Ellen G. White says, "The simplicity, the self-forgetfulness and the confiding love of a little child are the attributes that Heaven values" (*Desire of Ages*, 436).

In addition to the humility, simplicity, self-forgetfulness, and confiding love of little children, there are other things we can learn from them. Paulo Coelho, a Brazilian novelist, has observed closely how children go about life and says some of the things they do we can learn to do. He mentions three things children can teach adult people, namely

1. to have a joy without a reason;
2. to be busy with something all the time; and
3. to demand—with all power—what they want.

If we truly became like little children, we can enter the kingdom of heaven and be greatest there. And we can also find happiness and contentment even while here on earth living the life that children live.

On Love and Friendship

THERE IS A beautiful poem written by Roy Croft that defines and talks about love and friendship. It's entitled "Love" and is one of America's best-loved poems.

> I love you, not only for what you are,
> But for what I am when I am with you.
> I love you, not only for what you have made of
>   yourself,
> But for what you are making of me.
> I love you for the part of me that you bring out;
> I love you for putting your hand into my
>   heaped-up heart
> And passing over all the foolish, weak things
> That you can't help dimly seeing there,
> And for drawing out into the light
> All the beautiful belongings that no one else had
>   looked
> Quite far enough to find.
> I love you because you are helping me to make
> Of the lumber of my life not a tavern but a
>   temple;
> Out of the works of my every day not a reproach
> But a song.
> I love you because you have done more than any
>   creed

Could have done to make me good,
And more than any fate could have done
To make me happy.

You have done it without a touch,
Without a word,
Without a sign.
You have done it by being yourself.
Perhaps that is what being a friend means,
After all.

If your love and friendship has meant these and all to someone, then you are a friend indeed. And remember, if no one has been this kind of a friend to you, you have Jesus, the dearest and best friend of all. Will you make him your friend?

One Year to Live

SOME TIME AGO, I preached a sermon about having a purpose for living and adding excitement and joy to life by setting goals that one could achieve in a lifetime. Looking at the responses, the following list emerged:

1. Organize a home Bible study group.
2. Read the Bible through.
3. Plant a church.
4. Donate funds to build a chapel in a third-world country.
5. Establish a ministry geared towards children and their needs.
6. Visit the Holy Land.
7. Climb Mt. Sinai.
8. Travel and see the world: the Pyramids, Eiffel Tower, Machu Picchu, etc.
9. Learn a new language.
10. Write a book.

This list looks pretty good and no doubt a few more may be added to it. The problem with goals, however, is that they get so easily relegated to the back burner by the tyranny of the urgent and the invariable nature of our workaday routines.

It might help if one day we are told we only have just one year to live. Then we will have to prioritize. We will only have so much time left to do the most important things in our lives. Perhaps we will only pick three on the list and focus on those things.

Come to think about it, no one is even guaranteed one year. Even tomorrow may not come. The wise man says, "Do not boast about tomorrow, for you do not know what a day may bring forth" (Proverbs 27:1).

Only today is what we have.

So go ahead and start working today on the goals you want to achieve. And as the Lord is merciful, he might even allow you time to do the rest on your list if it glorifies his name and results in the advancement of his kingdom on earth.

Say It Now

THERE IS A beautiful poem that talks about love and friendship. It was written by an anonymous author and is among America's best-loved poems. It tells us that to be a true friend, it is not enough to love them. We need to show that love in our words and actions in much the same way that Jesus the true friend did. And we need to show this love we have for them *now*.

> If you have a friend worth loving,
> Love him. Yes, and let him know
> That you love him, ere life's evening
> Tinge his brow with sunset glow.
> Why should good words ne'er be said
> Of a friend—till he is dead?
>
> If you hear a song that thrills you
> Sung by any child of song,
> Praise it. Do not let the singer
> Wait deserved praises long.
> Why should one who thrills your heart
> Lack the joy you may impart?
>
> If you hear a prayer that moves you
> By its humble, pleading tone
> Join it. Do not let the seeker
> Bow before his God alone.

Why should not your brother share
The strength of "two or three" in prayer?

If you see the hot tears falling
From a brother's weeping eyes,
Share them. And by kindly sharing
Own our kinship in the skies.
Why should anyone be glad
When a brother's heart is sad?

If a silvery laugh goes rippling
through the sunshine on his face,
Share it. 'Tis the wise man's saying—
for both joy and grief a place.
There's health and goodness in the mirth
In which an honest laugh has birth.

If your work is made more easy
By a friendly, helping hand,
Say so. Speak out bravely and truly
Ere the darkness veil the land.
Should a brother workman dear
Falter for a word of cheer?

Scatter thus your seeds of kindness
All enriching as you go.
Leave them. Trust the Harvest Giver;
He will make each seed to grow,
So until the happy end
Your life shall never lack a friend.

Twenty-Four Things to Remember... and One Thing to Never Forget

As WE GET older, we tend to be forgetful. In fact, we use age as an excuse for forgetting. For some, the words "senior moment" come in handy every time.

But there are certain things that we should always remember. And no matter how old we are, there are no excuses for forgetting them. Like the title suggests, these are things we should always remember. And this will result in a happy and contented life.

They are inspiring, Bible based, and very practical. Putting them into practice will bring back meaning and significance to our day-to-day lives and add joy not only to ourselves but to others that we come in contact with as well.

> Your presence is a present to the world.
> You're unique and one of a kind.
> Your life can be what you want it to be.
> Take the days just one at a time.
>
> Count your blessings, not your troubles.
> You'll make it through whatever comes along.
> Within you are so many answers.
> Understand, have courage, be strong.
>
> Don't put limits on yourself.
> So many dreams are waiting to be realized.

Decisions are too important to leave to chance.
Reach for your peak, your goal, and your prize.

Nothing wastes more energy than worrying.
The longer one carries a problem, the heavier it gets.
Don't take things too seriously.
Live a life of serenity, not a life of regrets.

Remember that a little love goes a long way.
Remember that a lot...goes forever.
Remember that friendship is a wise investment.
Life's treasures are people...together.

Realize that it's never too late.
Do ordinary things in an extraordinary way.
Have health and hope and happiness.
Take the time to wish upon a star.

And don't ever forget...
For even a day...
How very special you are.
May you find more happiness, joy and zest for living with these reminders.

God, Make Me a TV!

A PRIMARY SCHOOL teacher asked her students to write an essay about what they would like God to do for them. At the end of the day, while marking the essays, she read one that made her very emotional.

Her husband, who had just walked in, saw her crying and asked her, "What's going on?"

She answered, "Read this. It is one of my students' essays."

The essay went this way:

> Oh God, tonight I ask you for something very special. Make me into a television. I want to take its place and live like the TV in my house.
>
> I want to have my own special place and have my family around ME. I want to be taken seriously when I talk. I want to be the center of attention and be heard without interruptions or questions. I want to receive the same special care that the TV receives even when it is not working. I want to have the company of my dad when he arrives home from work, even when he is tired. And I want my mom to want me when she is sad and upset, instead of ignoring me. And I want my brothers to fight to be with me.
>
> I want my family to just leave everything aside, every now and then, just to spend some time with me.

And last but not least, I want to ensure that
I can make them all happy and be able to entertain them. Lord I don't ask you for much. I just
want You to help me live my life like a TV.

At that moment, the husband said, "My god, poor kid. What
horrible parents!"

The wife looked up at him and said, "That essay is our son's!"

Regrettably today, the TV (or the smart phone or iPad or tablet)
has become the center of everything in many a home and in many a
child's life. Let us do what we can to give God his rightful place and
the things of eternal value their proper position in our homes and in
our hearts.

The A–Z of Managing Stress

HERE ARE SOME tips on how to manage stress that I came across and that I want to share with you as I believe they could be a big help. So many people today suffer from high blood pressure, stroke, heart attack, and other stress-related illnesses. Church-going people and even ministers and others in service-oriented professions especially suffer from stress and burnout.

We can be benefitted by trying out some of these suggestions.

Always take time for yourself with at least thirty minutes each day.

Be aware of your own stress meter. Know when to step back and cool down.

Concentrate on controlling your own situation without controlling everybody else.

Daily strenuous exercise burns off the stress chemicals in the body.

Eat lots of fresh fruit, veggies, and grains and drink plenty of water. Give your body the best for it to perform at its best.

Forgive others and don't hold grudges. Be tolerant—not everyone is as capable as you.

Gain perspective on things. How important is the issue? Choose your battles.

Hugs, kisses, and laughter. Have fun, and don't be afraid to share your feelings with others.

Identify stress situations and plan to deal with them better next time.

Judge your own performance realistically. Don't set goals that are way out of your own reach.

Keep a positive attitude. Your outlook will influence the way others treat you.

Limit if not totally eliminate alcohol, drugs, and other stimulants. They affect your perception and behavior.

Manage your money well. Seek expert advice and save at least 10 percent of what you earn.

"No" is a word you need to learn to use without feeling guilty.

Outdoor activities by yourself, or with friends and family, can be a great way to relax.

Play your favorite music instead of watching television.

Quit smoking. It is stressing your body and killing you slowly.

Relationships. Nurture and enjoy them. Learn to listen more and talk less.

Sleep well. Going to bed early and having seven to eight hours of restful sleep in a well-ventilated room can make the difference in your day.

Treating yourself once a week with a massage, dinner out, or watching a good movie can help relieve stress and slows down the dizzying pace of life.

Understand things from the other person's point of view.

Verify all information from the source before exploding.

Worry less. It does not get things done better or quicker.

Xpress. Regularly retreat to your favorite space
and make vacations part of your yearly plan
and budget.
Yearly goal setting. Plan what you want to achieve
based on your priorities in your personal life,
career, and relationships.
Zest for life. Each day is a gift from God. Smile
and be thankful by living it up and using it
to honor him and bless others.

Of course, Jesus said it best when he said not to worry (about tomorrow) for tomorrow will worry about its own things (Matthew 6:34).

And Paul advises, "Be anxious for nothing, but in everything by prayer and supplication, with thanksgiving, let your request be made known to God. And the peace of God, which passes all understanding, will guard your hearts and minds through Christ Jesus" (Philippians 4:6–7).

Forty Ways to a Fuller, Healthier, and Happier Life

AT THE BEGINNING of each year, we usually make some resolutions and map out strategies that would help us achieve these goals. And not long after, we find ourselves derailed, and things we have hoped for and dreamed about become just a distant memory.

Of course, we can always start all over. There is such a place called "a place of beginning again." After all, each new day is the first day of the rest of our lives.

From a site called Health Inspirations, I picked up some materials that I think are very good and a "must share" with everyone. They address life and the simple things we can do to live a better, healthier, and happier life. I know that if we take these seriously and do as suggested, it will make a difference in the way we live. We can enjoy life to the fullest and can be a greater blessing to those around us.

Jesus didn't only purchase the gift of eternal life for us. He also made it possible for us to have an abundant life here and now. He said, "I am come that they might have life and that they might have it more abundantly" (John 10:10).

And if we want to enjoy this gift, we need to work at it. The following suggestions will surely help:

1. Realize that life is a school, and you are here to learn. Problems are simply part of the curriculum that appear and fade away like algebra class, but the lessons you learn will last a lifetime.

2. Walk or jog for ten to thirty minutes each day.
3. No one is in charge of your happiness except you.
4. Sleep for eight hours a day.
5. Dream more while you are awake.
6. Don't waste your precious energy on gossip.
7. Make peace with your past so it won't spoil your present.
8. Get rid of anything that isn't useful, beautiful, and joyful.
9. Don't overdo. Keep your limits.
10. Enjoy life each moment. Try new things.
11. Love yourself because you are unique and wonderful in your own way.
12. Sit in silence for at least ten minutes each day.
13. Make time to practice meditation and prayer every day.
14. Read more books than you did last month.
15. Eat breakfast like a king, lunch like a prince, and dinner like a pauper.
16. However good or bad a situation is, it will change.
17. Call your family often.
18. What other people think of you is none of your business.
19. When you awake alive in the morning, thank God for it.
20. The best is yet to come.
21. Eat more foods that grow on trees and plants and eat less food that is manufactured in plants.
22. Try to make at least three people smile each day.
23. Smile and laugh more.
24. Forgive everyone for everything.
25. Your innermost is always happy. So be happy.
26. Live with the three E's: energy, enthusiasm, and empathy.
27. Drink plenty of water, at least two liters each day.
28. Forget issues of the past. Don't remind your partner with his or her mistakes of the past.
29. You don't have to win every argument. Agree to disagree.
30. Time heals everything.
31. Don't take yourself too seriously. No one else does.
32. Don't have negative thoughts or things you cannot control. Instead, invest your energy in the positive present moment.

33. Your job won't take care of you when you are sick. Your friends will. Stay in touch.
34. Envy is a waste of time. You already have all you need or definitely will get what you really, really want.
35. Life is too short to waste time hating anyone, so get rid of those ill feelings.
36. Each day, do something good to others.
37. Spend more time with people over the age of seventy and under the age of six.
38. Don't compare your life to anyone. You have no idea what their journey is all about.
39. Play more games.
40. No matter how you feel, get up, dress up, and show up.

I wish for you the best, and I pray God grants us his providential leading as we continue our journey through the year and through the rest of our lives.

A Cure for Burnout

IN BITS AND Pieces, January 7, 1993, the "Coronary and Ulcer Club" lists the following rules for members, somewhat in a tongue-and-cheek way:

1. Your job comes first. Forget everything else.
2. Saturdays, Sundays, and holidays are fine times to be working at the office. There will be nobody else there to bother you.
3. Always have your briefcase with you when not at your desk. This provides an opportunity to review completely all the troubles and worries of the day.
4. Never say "no" to a request. Always say "yes."
5. Accept all invitations to meetings, banquets, committees, etc.
6. All forms of recreation are a waste of time.
7. Never delegate responsibility to others; carry the entire load yourself.
8. If your work calls for traveling, work all day and travel at night to keep that appointment you made for eight the next morning.
9. No matter how many jobs you already are doing, remember you always can take on more.

If we follow these rules as suggested by the club, we will have coronary problems, ulcers, and suffer burnout in no time. It also goes without saying that when we do the opposite of these rules, our health and happiness will improve.

So let's do it the other way for it is God's plan that we accomplish his will in our lives in the best way possible. He says in the scriptures, "Beloved, I wish above all things that thou mayest prosper and be in health, even as thy soul prospereth" (3 John 2).

A Memorable Golden Anniversary Celebration

I JUST ARRIVED from a nine-day trip to the Philippines where I participated in the celebration of the fiftieth foundation anniversary of Tirad View Academy in Quirino, Ilocos Sur. It was a memorable experience as I returned to a place I haven't visited in thirty years.

A number of things impressed me. First was the means of travel that has improved so much. In our day, it would take at least a day to get there from the mission headquarters in Baguio. And if anything happened with the truck, you may have to wait till the next day to get there. This time, we left Baguio at 3:30 a.m. and got into the school grounds in time for the parade and the program that started at 8:00 a.m.

It was also great to see a lot of alumni coming home for the celebrations. Some came from Austria, Germany, England, the United States, the Middle East, the Far East, and from all over the Philippines. This alone speaks volumes in terms of school spirit and loyalty and the depth of friendship formed while in attendance at this Christian institution.

I was impressed at the new structures that have been built and are in the process of construction like the administration building/auditorium, library, elementary school building, girl's dormitory, and alumni center/guest house. And to know that these projects have been built not from funds coming from the organization but from the generosity of individual alumni and friends and supporters of the school.

What has impressed me the most was the fact that many of those I had the privilege of knowing and teaching for a brief period of time are now leaders in their own right today. Some of them are now principals and members of the faculty and staff, district pastors, and community leaders. A number of them shared with me something I said or did at one time in the past, and that I have long forgotten, but that made a difference in their lives and has given them the courage to press on till they achieved success.

And by the way, this was also the place where thirty-nine years ago, I was ordained into the gospel ministry. And my visit gave me a golden opportunity to renew my commitment to the call to gospel work and be faithful to the task till the very end.

I think about that grand reunion in heaven. There will be those who will come and remind us of the things we said and things we did that inspired them and gave the lift they needed in their spiritual journey.

And like Paul, we should determine to "keep under my body and bring it unto subjection lest after I have preached to others, I myself will be a castaway" (1 Corinthians 9:27).

A Meaningful or a Happy Life?

IN HIS BOOK, *Man's Search for Meaning*, Victor Frankl, a prominent Jewish psychiatrist and neurologist who worked in a Vienna hospital giving wrong diagnoses to mentally ill patients to save them from being euthanized by the ruling Nazis, talks about the importance of meaning and purpose in life as the key to surviving all odds.

He and his pregnant wife together with his parents were arrested and transported to the concentration camp in September 1942, and the book chronicles the horrors, atrocities, and horrific conditions that he and others experienced at the camps. Liberation came three years later, but by that time, thousands have perished, including his wife and most of his family. Frankl then suggests that the difference between those that survived and those that perished could be explained by one thing: meaning. Those that had meaning and purpose in life survived while those who lost their purpose in living simply gave up.

Frankl's message is obviously at odds with our culture that is more interested in the pursuit of happiness than in the search for meaning. In America, our immediate needs are so well met yet according to the Center for Disease Prevention and Control, about four out of ten Americans have not discovered a satisfying life purpose.

In a study published by the *Journal of Positive Psychology*, psychological scientists asked some four hundred Americans whether they thought their lives were meaningful and/or happy. The researchers found that happy people get joy from receiving while people leading meaningful lives get joy from giving to others. The authors write, "Happiness without meaning characterizes a relatively shallow, self-absorbed, or even selfish life, in which things go well, needs and desire are easily satisfied, and difficult and taxing entanglements are avoided."

The researchers also discovered that people who are happy have a tendency to think that life is easy, are in good physical health, and are able to buy the things they need. Happiness is defined by a lack of stress or worry. They point out, however, that humans are not the only ones who can feel happy. Animals also feel happy when their needs and drives are satisfied. Therefore, what sets human beings apart from animals is not the pursuit of happiness but the pursuit of meaning.

Was this not the kind of life that Jesus came to live—a life of meaning that he also desires for every follower of his to live by? It was not just a happy life that Jesus lived and promises to give but a life full of meaning and purpose.

He said, "Even as the Son of Man came not to be ministered unto but to minister and to give His life a ransom for many" (Matthew 20:28).

A Pound of Butter

THERE WAS A farmer who sold a pound of butter to the baker. One day, the baker decided to weigh the butter to see if he was getting a pound, and he found that he was not. This angered him, and he took the farmer to court. The judge asked the farmer if he was using any measure.

The farmer replied, "Your Honor, I am primitive. I don't have a proper measure, but I do have a scale."

The judge asked, "Then how do you weigh the butter?"

The farmer replied, "Your Honor, long before the baker started buying butter from me, I have been buying a pound loaf of bread from him. Every day when the baker brings the bread, I put it on the scale and give him the same weight in butter. If anyone is to be blamed, it is the baker."

What is the moral of the story?

"We get back in life what we give to others."

The scriptures say, "Be not deceived, God is not mocked: for whatsoever a man soweth, that shall he also reap" (Galatians 6:7). And Matthew 7:2 says, "And with what measure you mete, it shall be measured to you again."

Whenever you take an action, ask yourself this question: Am I giving fair value for the wages or money I hope to make? Honesty and dishonesty become a habit. Some people practice dishonesty and can lie with a straight face. Others lie so much that they don't even know what the truth is anymore. But who are they deceiving? Themselves.

Alive or Dead?

THE FOLLOWING MATERIAL written by an anonymous author gives more of the identifying marks of an individual or a church that is dead or alive.

If we see that we are more on the dead church side, it is time to heed the advice of the Lord Jesus. And that is to be watchful, hold fast and repent (Revelation 3:2, 3).

Live churches' expenses are always more than their income; dead churches don't need much money!

Live churches have parking problems; dead churches have empty spaces!

Live churches may have some noisy children; dead churches are quiet as a cemetery.

Live churches keep changing their ways of doing things; dead churches see no need for change!

Live churches grow so fast you can't keep up with people's names; in dead churches, everybody knows everybody's name.

Live churches strongly support world missions; dead churches keep the money at home!

Live churches are full of regular, cheerful givers; dead churches are full of grudging tippers!

Live churches move ahead on prayer and faith; dead churches work only on sight!

Live churches plant daughter churches; dead churches fear spending the money, time, and talent!

Live churches outgrow their facilities; dead churches have room to spare!

Live churches welcome all classes of people; dead churches stick to their own kind!

Live churches' members read their Bibles and bring them to church; dead churches' members seldom do!

Live churches' members enthusiastically support the ministries; dead churches have no ministries—only functions!

Live churches' members look for someone they can help; dead churches' members look for something to complain about!

Live churches' members reach out to share their faith in Christ; dead churches' members don't have enough to share!

I like the last one in particular. In fact, someone said that a church that doesn't live on its capture is on its way to the cemetery!

Amazing Gifts of Modern Medicine and Technology

As WE GOT back from the hospital and retired for the night, I looked back at the day's events, and I couldn't thank God enough for what he had done. There were difficult and impossible challenges, but God took control, and we praised his holy name.

Earlier in the day, we took the two-and-a-half-hour drive from Los Angeles to San Diego to be a support to our daughter and son-in-law, Jane and Carlo. Their daughter Ella Jules was born prematurely, and she had already been almost three weeks in the hospital. Being only a twenty-four-week-term baby, she had to be given the utmost care in terms of treatment and nourishment to develop her vital organs into their normal and full condition.

The doctors reported a hole in her heart, as is common with "preemies." This was causing her blood pressure to elevate and her heart to work a lot harder than usual. For almost three weeks, they tried to close the hole through medication. But it wasn't working, and not wanting to continue to burden her heart unnecessarily and pose a risk to her other organs, the doctors recommended surgery.

We saw her wheeled out of her room with an entourage of nurses, medical gadgets, and the rest of the surgical team. We engaged in more praying as we awaited the results. Two hours later, we saw the face of her surgeon beaming as he returned to give his report. It was a successful procedure. The baby did great. When we were later allowed into her room, we saw that all her vital signs were good, including her blood pressure that her surgeon noticed went back to normal immediately after the hole in her heart was clipped.

The devotional we were reading that day was a source of great spiritual strength, and it came on with a special meaning.

Jeremiah 32:27 says, "I am the Lord, the God of all mankind. Is anything too hard for me?" And we can say through our experience that day, as we have already proven so many times in our lives, truly nothing is too difficult for him. Actually, there is nothing impossible for him. What we see as difficult is easy with him. The impossible just takes a little bit longer.

As we left the hospital that night, we made our last visit with our little baby. She was still sedated from the procedure as she was going to be all night. But she lay quietly and peacefully in the incubator because someone was tenderly watching over her. Jeremiah's words rang so clearly again, "For I know the plans I have for you," declares the Lord, "plans to prosper you and not to harm you, plans to give you hope and a future" (Jeremiah 29:11).

An Eighty-Year-Old Mom's Letter to Her Children on Her Birthday

IN A LETTER that was written by an eighty-year-old mother to her children on her birthday, she expresses what gifts she wishes to receive from them. It's a material that was read by Dr. James Dobson on a *Focus on the Family* radio broadcast.

The letter reads as follows:

> To all my children:
>
> I suppose my upcoming birthday started my thoughts along these lines… This is a good time to tell you that what I truly want are things I can never get enough of, yet they are free. I want the intangibles.
>
> I would like for you to come and sit with me, and for you to be relaxed. We can talk, or we can be silent. I would just like for us to be together.
>
> I need your patience when I don't hear what you say the first time. I know how tiresome it is to always be repeating, but sometimes I must ask you to repeat. I need your patience when I think too much about the past, with my slowness and my set ways. I want you to be tolerant with what the years have done to me physically.

Please be understanding about my personal care habits. I spill things. I lose things. I get unduly excited when I try to figure out my bank statements. I can't remember what time to take my medication, or if I took it already. I take too many naps. Sometimes sleep helps to pass the day.

Well, there you have it: Time, Patience, and Understanding. These are priceless gifts that I want.

Finally, in his letter, the Apostle Paul wrote, "I can do all things through Christ which strengtheneth me." I know I can, too! It's a wonderful feeling to know His eye is on the sparrow and I know He cares for me. I guess being old isn't so bad after all!

Love,
Mom

Oh sure, they appreciate the flowers, the special meal, the purse, and other expensive gifts we choose for them. But more precious than these are the gifts of time, patience, and understanding we can offer them as they struggle with the onset of the years. And to think that they gave so much of these to us through our growing up years should make us give these intangible gifts to them with the deepest of our love and gratitude.

Be Positive and the World Will Be Yours

OUR ATTITUDE DETERMINES to a large degree the amount of success or failure we achieve in life. As someone has aptly said, "Your attitude determines your altitude."

So we need to stay positive and never allow anything negative to pull us down as we journey through life. And even when things get so bleak, we can still find something to buoy us up if we try.

I read recently about two boys who were born into the same family who had directly opposite personalities. One was a hopeless pessimist while the other was an incorrigible optimist.

One Christmas, the dad did something to test them. Late on Christmas Eve, the dad unloaded a large bag of toys in the room of the pessimist son while he dumped horse manure in the room of the other. When the pessimist son woke up in the morning and saw all the toys in his room, he went into a corner sobbing and complaining that he would get tired reading all the instruction manuals of the toys he got. The optimist son on the other hand was awakened by the smell of horse manure, and he jumped out of bed in search of a pony—which would possibly be the best Christmas gift he would ever get thus far.

So be positive, and here are a few tips on being one so that we could sail smoothly into our dreams.

1. Never respond when you are not calm. If you are not sure that you are calm, don't respond. Take time to calm yourself down first.

2. Take a deep breath as a first step to calm yourself down.
3. Speak in gentle tone to reduce the tension of the situation.
4. Realize that you can find opportunities in negative situations. Albert Einstein said, "In the middle of every difficulty lies opportunity."
5. Look at the content of what people say to you for something positive that you can act upon to improve yourself. Don't just reject the whole messages.
6. For the rest of the messages that are negative, simply ignore them.
7. Maintain a positive view of the people. Maybe you don't like their messages or behavior, but that doesn't mean that you can hate them personally.
8. Realize that having negative feelings will just hurt you, not them. So there is no reason for you to have any negative feeling.
9. If you make mistakes, be open to admit it.
10. If you make mistakes, remember this quote: "A life spent making mistakes is not only more honorable, but more useful than a life spent doing nothing."
11. If you can, listen to motivational audio program to feed positive thoughts into your mind.
12. Talk to a positive friend who can encourage you.

Do We Really Believe When We Pray?

JESUS TOLD HIS disciples that one of the prerequisites of answered prayer is faith. He said, "And all things, whatsoever ye shall ask in prayer, believing, ye shall receive" (Matthew 21:22).

Too many of us though pray and ask God for blessings, great and small. And yet, we are unbelieving; thus many of our petitions are denied. God is so gracious; however, sometimes he grants our requests in spite of our unbelief. A classic Bible example of this was the early church when they prayed for the release of Peter who at the time was in jail. When the apostle showed up at the door of the house where the church was praying, following his miraculous escape from prison with the help of God's special angel, none of the believers would take the girl's word who told them she saw Peter standing at the door. They thought she saw a ghost!

There is a more modern story that sadly points out this unbelief-in-prayer mind-set. In a small town that had historically been "dry," a local businessman decided to build a tavern. A group of Christians from a local church were concerned and planned an all-night prayer meeting to ask God to intervene.

It so happened that shortly thereafter, lightning struck the bar, and it burned to the ground. The owner of the bar sued the church, claiming that the prayers of the congregation were responsible, but the church hired a lawyer to argue in court that they were not responsible. After his initial review of the case, the presiding judge stated that "no matter how this case comes out, one thing is clear. The tavern owner believes in prayer, and the Christians do not."

If we were more believing, there would be more answers to our prayers. Let us believe because time and time again, Jesus said, "According to your faith be it unto you" (Matthew 9:29).

Celebrate Today

IF YOU ARE like most people, you probably stay up till midnight to join the millions on television welcome the New Year at New York's Times Square and the hundreds of thousands more who celebrate by watching Pasadena's Rose Parade. I watch some TV myself during these occasions, and at times, newscasters show clips of how people celebrate the New Year in Tokyo, London, Moscow, and other great cities of the world.

The New Year comes at different times to different people, particularly the Romans, the Jews, the Chinese, and other nationalities. But regardless of when the New Year begins, people like to bring it in with a bang. And this is so because the New Year is a symbol of hope. It provides opportunity to start anew. If people messed up during the year that is past, the New Year gives them a chance to shape up and straighten their lives. If they did well in the previous year, they have an opportunity to do even better.

But consider the following statement: "Today is the first day of the rest of your life." This is all so true, and it is also true that each day that comes is a symbol of hope. It is also a time to begin anew. If you messed up yesterday, you can redeem yourself today. And if you did well yesterday, you can do even better today.

A quote from the Sanskrit says, "Yesterday is but a dream and tomorrow a vision, but today well lived makes every yesterday a dream of happiness and every tomorrow a vision of hope. Look well, therefore,. to this day."

The wise man says, "Do not boast about tomorrow for you do not know what tomorrow may bring forth" (Proverbs 27:1). Jesus himself says, "Do not worry about tomorrow, for tomorrow will take care of itself; sufficient unto the day is the evil thereof" (Matthew 6:34).

So today is all you have. It is God's gift to you, that's why it is called a "present." It is the first day of the rest of your life. It gives hope. It is a time to start anew and begin again. Celebrate it. Live well today and every day of your life.

Taking Care of Yourself

WE ARE REMINDED that we are here on earth to relieve the misery, the pain, and the suffering in the world around us. And the Lord has stated that he came into this world not to be served but to serve—and to give his life a ransom for many (Matthew 20:28). Those of us who are his followers are to do what he has done and live as he has lived. In fact, we are obligated to do this. This is what we are here on earth for. In the words of one, he says, "Service is the rent we pay for the space we occupy on earth."

But why is it that there are so many in the service professions who experience burnout. And why do we hear time and time again of people who are themselves the face of ministry and service suddenly breaking down or doing something reckless and crazy and bringing their careers to an abrupt end.

The answer may be found in the fact of one giving and giving and giving until nothing is left and the soul gets spiritually bankrupt with nothing more to give because one has not taken the time to replenish on a daily basis from the feet of him who is the source of all power and energy and strength.

When Jesus said that the second great commandment is to love one's neighbor as one loves oneself, (Matthew 19:19), he was implying that one has to take care of himself first so that he is able to love and take care of his neighbor. So caregivers and providers ought to give care for themselves first by staying connected to Jesus who is the vine and drawing life and power from him on a daily basis.

I also found something inspirational from a blog that calls itself Athens Voice, and here are some helpful suggestions on taking care of ourselves so we can better be able to care for others.

Twelve Steps to Self-Care
1. If it feels wrong, don't do it.
2. Say exactly what you mean.
3. Don't be a people pleaser.
4. Trust your instincts.
5. Never speak bad about yourself.
6. Never give up on your dreams.
7. Don't be afraid to say no.
8. Don't be afraid to say yes.
9. Be kind to yourself.
10. Let go of what you can't control
11. Stay away from drama and negativity.
12. LOVE.

Let's make sure our needs are taken care of. Then we are ready to care for the needs of our fellow travelers.

Christianity and the Home

SOMETIMES IN AN effort to keep up with our name and image, we do the best we can to put our best foot forward when in public or in the eyes of others. We do whatever it takes to live up to our reputation as refined, noble, and dignified individuals.

The problem is when we get home, and we are no longer in the public eye, we just slouch and drop our guard. We let go our defenses and do not care at all how we act. We are rough, unkind, and even rude to the people who deserve the best from us.

Ellen G. White under inspiration writes, "The religion of Christ will lead us to do all the good possible, to both high and low, rich and poor, happy and oppressed. But especially will it lead to the manifestation of kindness in our own family. It will be manifested by acts of courtesy and love to father and mother, husband, wife, and child. We are to look to Jesus, to catch His Spirit, to live in the light of His goodness and love, and to reflect His glory upon others" (My Life Today, 200.2).

In another place, she says Christianity makes a man a gentleman. In fact, if one is truly converted, his family would be the first to notice. And it is true that when this happens, even his dog will see the difference.

So as we give ourselves to Christ, let our connection with Christ be manifested in a loving, kind, and cheerful disposition to those that deserve the best from us and let this "streams of living water" (John 7:38) flow and spill far away into the world around us.

A True Friend

PROVERBS 17:17 DEFINES a friend as one who "loves at all times, and a brother is born for adversity." But what do you do when your friend falls into disfavor in the church, and everybody tries to avoid him because of sin or is perceived to have sinned? Do you still love him, or would you abandon him?

Our Savior hates sin, but he loves sinners. And one of the most difficult tasks we as Christians are asked to do is to love a sinner while at the same time hate his sin. This is hard to do unless we have Christ's love in our hearts. Christ is our example, and we are to follow Him.

When your friend is down and out, don't turn your back on him or deprive him of your uplifting Christ-like influence.

The best picture ever portrayed of a true friend is the one that says, "A friend is one who walks in when the whole world walks out."

A story is told of Chuck Colson who spent time in prison for his part in the Watergate debacle. When he got out of prison, he wrote a book entitled *Born Again*. In this book, he narrated a story of his experience with many encounters with students on various university campus lectures.

Students hated Nixon and everybody associated with Nixon, and so he was bombarded with many pointed and vitriolic questions. One student stood up and read Henry Kissinger's criticism of Nixon.

Then he asked, "Mr. Colson, do you agree with Kissinger's criticism of Nixon?"

Colson replied, "Mr. Nixon's negative traits of character has been dissected more than anybody I know, and it is almost universally known that I don't see any need to add to what have already been made public. Mr. Nixon is my friend, and I don't turn my back on my friend."

Mr. Colson was given a standing ovation even by those who hated him and Mr. Nixon. Nobody likes anybody who turns their back on their friend.

The best friend you can ever have is JESUS. He is a true friend. He never turns his back on you.

Commitment Needed

THE STORY IS told that when Julius Caesar landed on the shores of Britain with his Roman legions, he took a bold and decisive step to ensure the success of his military venture.

Ordering his men to march to the edge of the Cliffs of Dover, he commanded them to look down at the water below. To their amazement, they saw every ship in which they had crossed the channel engulfed in flames. Caesar had deliberately cut off any possibility of retreat.

Now that his soldiers were unable to return to the continent, there was nothing left for them to do but to advance and conquer! And that is exactly what they did.

In the Christian life, we too need to burn our bridges and leave no connection with the old life or the world that we have lived in. Jesus said, "No one, having put his hand to the plow, and looking back, is fit for the kingdom of God" (Luke 9:68).

Commitment, focus, and singleness of purpose are what we need if we have to be successful in following Christ. In fact, this is what is going to give us complete satisfaction and genuine happiness as we journey to our heavenly home.

Don't Jump to Conclusions

A LITTLE GIRL was holding an apple in each of her hands. Her mom came in and asked her daughter, "Sweetie, could you give your mom one of your apples?"

The girl looked up at her mom for a few seconds and then took a quick bite on one apple, and quickly on the other.

The smile on the mother's face froze. She bit her lips and tried hard not to show her disappointment.

But then the little girl handed one of the apples to her mom and then said, "Mommy, here you are. This is the sweeter one."

In life, we sometimes experience needless hurt and dismay because we are quick to assume and make premature judgments. The fact is, no matter who we are, or how experienced and knowledgeable we think we are, it pays to always delay judgment. Give others the privilege to explain themselves. What we see may not be the reality. So never jump into conclusions.

Isn't this why Jesus said in his Sermon on the Mount, "Judge not that you be not judged"? (Matthew 7:1). Only God can judge righteously because only he knows all the circumstances surrounding a particular situation, and he alone can read the heart.

Do Not Wait Till You Lose Your Friend

FRIENDSHIPS AND FAMILY relationships are of great value in our lives. They contribute much to the quality and the quantity of our years. Studies and personal experiences show that we can have much more enjoyable, exciting, and longer-lasting lives when we have these blessings surrounding us.

Then let's spend time with our families and friends. Let us cultivate and nurture these relationships and keep them in good repair. Let's not wait until we lose them, and only then would we realize how much they really meant to us.

Here's a poem by Henson Towne that is a good read and a reminder to us all about giving priority to maintaining our relationships:

Around the Corner

Around the corner I have a friend,
In this great city that has no end.
Yet days go by and weeks rush on,
And before I know it a year is gone,
And I never see my old friend's face;
For life is a swift and terrible race.

He knows I like him just as well
As in the days when I rang his bell
And he rang mine. We were younger then—

And now we are busy, tired men—
Tired with playing a foolish game;
Tired with trying to make a name.

"Tomorrow," I say, "I will call on Jim,
Just to show that I'm thinking of him."
But tomorrow comes—and tomorrow goes;
And the distance between us grows and grows.
Around the corner!—yet miles away…

"Here's a telegram, sir."
"Jim died today."
And that's what we get—and deserve in the end—
Around the corner, a vanished friend.

God bless us all, and may we truly appreciate what a blessing
friends and families are in our lives while we still have them.

Twenty Words That Can Change Your Life

I WANT TO share with you a very good motivational material sent to me by a friend through music video. I am sure these words will assist you in making changes in your life for the better. Here are the following:

1. BEGIN. Take charge of your life by beginning something you have always wanted to do. If your goal seems overwhelming, start small.
2. IMAGINE. Your imagination has no boundaries. Dreaming about something is the first step toward achieving it.
3. LAUGH. Laughter is a direct route to the soul. It broadens your perspective, keeps you healthy, and makes an unbearable situation easier to deal with.
4. BELIEVE. Set your mind to predict success. Tell yourself you *will* succeed at whatever you're doing at the moment.
5. SEEK. Allow yourself to grow by exposing your vulnerability and insecurity. Don't live strictly inside your comfort zone. Don't always play it safe.
6. PLAY. We can always find something that can be done, and we forget how to have fun. Make conscious effort to take time off. You'll feel refreshed and able to think more clearly afterward.
7. TRUST. Being paralyzed by indecision is worse than making the wrong decision. You can't grow if you don't trust your inner voice.

8. LISTEN. Try listening to the other person's point of view first without being preoccupied or distracted. You'll really hear what is being said, and the other person is more likely to pay attention to your view.

9. CREATE. Creativity maintains the balance in our lives. The more we use our creativity, the more it develops.

10. CONNECT. Relationships are what pull us through the hard times and make the good times meaningful. Take the time to nurture the connections that uplift you.

11. TOUCH. Humans need touch to survive and thrive. Don't forget to hug your loved ones. Pat your friends on the back literally and figuratively.

12. FORGIVE. Forgiveness is life-giving because it puts you in charge. You become empowered.

13. PRAY. Prayer is asking God to transform the situation and become the heart of your life. Take time each day to talk to him.

14. HOPE. Hope is the knowledge that even in the worst of times we can triumph over hardship and sorrow and grow in spirit. Hope is what sustains humanity.

15. CHOOSE. We can't always choose our circumstances, but we can choose our attitudes toward them.

16. APPRECIATE. Admire the good in yourself and in those around you.

17. GIVE. Happiness involves giving freely to others and not necessarily wanting something in return.

18. READ. Reading removes boundaries.

19. WRITE. Words help preserve and sustain freedom. Words are power.

20. RELEASE. Avoid doing something just because everyone thinks you should. Give yourself permission to relax.

These are impact words—words that have the power to change the direction of your life, from aimlessness to a sense of purpose, from futility to usefulness, from the threshold of failure to the pavilion of success. Give heed to them, even if you have to go by just one word each day in your life.

Focus on their meaning, treasure them in your heart, live by them, and then go ahead and prime yourself for abundant living the rest of your life.

The Porcupine Story

IT WAS THE coldest winter ever. Many animals died because of the cold. The porcupines, realizing the situation, decided to group together to keep warm. This way they covered and protected themselves, but the quills of each one wounded their closest companions.

After a while, they decided to distance themselves one from the other. But one by one they began to die, alone and frozen.

So they had to make a choice: either accept the quills of their companions or disappear from the earth. Wisely, they decided to go back to being together. They learned to live with the little wounds caused by the close relationship with their companions in order to receive the warmth that came from the others. This way, they were able to survive.

This story shows us that the best relationships do not happen when perfect people are staying together, but they occur when each individual learns to live with the imperfections of others and get to admire the other person's good qualities.

Yes, we can *learn to live with the pricks in our lives*. It is a testimony to the power of the gospel and the work of the Holy Spirit in our lives. We get blessed with happiness, peace, and joy. And God himself is glorified.

The psalmist declares, "Behold how good and how pleasant it is for brethren to dwell together in unity!" (Psalm 133:1).

Friends and Your Health

AT THE TIRE store where I waited to have new tires mounted on my car, I picked up a magazine, and one article fascinated me. It basically dealt with the effect of friends and social relationships to one's health and general well-being.

The material cited two studies done in 2010 at the University of Chicago that showed how loneliness leads to depression and lethargy. It also mentions how in 2013 British researchers have discovered that large social networks bolster one's health and general well-being.

These findings tell us something. If we want to be healthy and have a sense of well-being, we need to cultivate our friendships. Strengthen the ties and renew the bonds that have held us together in the past. Take the relationships we have and bring them to the next level. Casual acquaintances become friends, and ordinary friends turn into the best of friends.

And of course, there should be room for new ones. If you go out looking for new friends, there should be plenty around. The article suggests three things you can do to make it happen.

1.   Talk to strangers. Many of us are scared and too shy to talk to strangers. This could be a carryover of that safety warning from kindergarten: "never talk to strangers." But we are grown-ups. And especially when you see these new faces at church, at weddings, at funerals, and other functions. You will find out that these people are looking for a group

they can belong to or are there because they share the same interests and concerns that you do.

2. Take risks. We are afraid of rejection. We don't want to barge into people's conversations and ruin their evening. But you can always politely get out and simply move on. There is also the point of vulnerability. To the degree you are willing to share of yourself, to that level the relationship deepens in intimacy. And you will reach a point where the friendship develops into the party committing to cover your back while you pledge the same.

3. Choose your mission. When you have developed a purpose in life, and you go ahead and pursue that quest, you will meet people. Sometimes, you will need to form or organize groups for the purpose of achieving your goals. And in the process, friendships develop as a by-product.

Health and happiness do not come by our staying at home by ourselves. We need to go out there where the people are. As we bless them with our love and friendship, they too will bless us with theirs, and this will result in a healthier, happier world. The scripture suggests, "A man who has friends must himself be friendly, but there is a friend who sticks closer than a brother" (Proverbs 18:24).

Ten Commandments for the Family

IT HAS BEEN said that as the family goes, so does society. And that's because the family unit is the most basic and the most fundamental of social institutions. So should we not do everything we can to strengthen the family unit in order to affect society and make it what heaven plans it to be?

The following are Ten Commandments for the family that when followed will make this world a better place to live in.

1. Thou shalt laugh and play together.
2. Thou shalt worship and pray together.
3. Thou shalt share household responsibilities.
4. Thou shalt have family meals regularly.
5. Thou shalt appreciate each other's differences.
6. Thou shalt speak openly about thy needs.
7. Thou shalt listen with thy heart.
8. Thou shalt generously give and forgive.
9. Thou shalt celebrate thy heritage and tradition.
10. Thou shalt say "I love you" every day.

Each One Has a Story

A TWENTY-FOUR-YEAR-OLD BOY looking out from the train's window shouted, "Dad, look...the trees are going behind us!"

The father smiled while a young couple seated nearby looked at the twenty-four-year-old's childish behavior with pity.

Suddenly, he again exclaimed, "Dad, look...the clouds are running with us!"

The couple couldn't resist anymore and said to the old man, "Why don't you take your son to a good doctor?"

The old man smiled and said, "I did, and we just came from the hospital. You see, my son was blind from birth. He just got his eyes today."

Every single person on the planet has a story. Don't judge people before you truly know them. The truth might surprise you.

That's why Jesus said, "Judge not that you be not judged" (Matthew 7:1). We cannot see the heart. We do not know their story. Like one man who determined to never judge anyone by what he sees "until he has walked a mile in his moccasins." We shall never be able to rightly understand someone until we have lived his life and shared his journey, felt his joys, experienced his sorrows, knew his pain, and understood his glory.

When we do as Jesus commands, we will discover the truth at its very core. More than likely we will find ourselves empathizing with people rather than patronizing, admiring them rather than vilifying, applauding them rather than despising, and cherishing them rather than loathing.

Let us join others as they celebrate the blessings of life no matter how simple they may seem to be. Some of them may just have gotten their eyes.

Enjoying Life at Every Moment

A FISHERMAN WAS sitting near the seashore, in the shade of a tree whiling the time away. A businessman passing by approached him and asked why he was there doing nothing. In response, the fisherman replied that he had already caught enough fish for the day.

His reply upset the rich man who said, "Why don't you go catch more fish instead of sitting in the shade wasting your time?"

"What would I do with the fish that I catch?" the fisherman asked.

The businessman answered, "You could sell them, earn more money, and buy a bigger boat.

The fisherman asked, "What would I do then?"

The businessman replied, "You could go fishing in deep waters and catch even more fish and earn even more money."

The fisherman asked, "What would I do then?"

The businessman said, "You could buy more boats, have people work for you, and earn even more money."

The fisherman replied, "What would I do then?"

The businessman answered, "You could become a rich businessman like me."

The fisherman asked, "What would I do then?"

The businessman replied, "You could then relax and enjoy life."

Then the fisherman said, "What do you think I'm doing right now?"

As the simple fisherman observed, happiness in life doesn't consist in riches and material wealth. It is found in the simple things in life, in the absence of worry, in not having so many wants and desires for the things of this world. It is found in contentment and peace and in the enjoyment of each moment that comes.

Jesus said, "A man's life consists not in the abundance of things that he possesses" (Luke 12:15). Real happiness in life is found in knowing that one is safe in God's hands and is an heir to the riches of his grace and the blessings of citizenship in his eternal kingdom.

No Right to Keep It to Ourselves

FRITZ KREISLER (1875–1962), the world-famous violinist, earned a fortune with his concerts and compositions, but he generously gave most of it away. So when he discovered an exquisite violin on one of his trips, he wasn't able to buy it.

Later, having raised enough money to meet the asking price, he returned to the seller, hoping to purchase that beautiful instrument. But to his great dismay, it had been sold to a collector.

Kreisler made his way to the new owner's home and offered to buy the violin. The collector said it had become his prized possession, and he would not sell it.

Keenly disappointed, Kreisler was about to leave when he had an idea. "Could I play the instrument once more before it is consigned to silence?" he asked.

Permission was granted, and the great virtuoso filled the room with such heart-moving music that the collector's emotions were deeply stirred.

"I have no right to keep that to myself," he exclaimed. "It's yours, Mr. Kreisler. Take it into the world, and let people hear it."

We too have been given a most important message: God sent his Son into the world to die for us, and anyone who believes in him will never perish but will have everlasting life (John 3:16).

This precious message has been graciously given to us. But we have no right to keep it to ourselves. In the world of God's saving grace, we are musicians more than collectors. We need to go and share it with others. And let the world ring with the music of God's grace.

How Much Stuff Do We Really Need?

IN THE FIFTH century, a man named Arenius determined to live a holy life. So he abandoned the comforts of Egyptian society to follow an austere lifestyle in the desert. Yet whenever he visited the great city of Alexandria, he spent time wandering through its bazaars. Asked why, he explained that his heart rejoiced at the sight of all the things he didn't need (*Our Daily Bread* 1994).

Those of us who live in a society flooded with consumer goods and high-tech gadgets need to consider the example of that desert dweller of olden times. A typical supermarket in the United States in 1976 stocked nine thousand articles; today it may carry as much as forty thousand. But how many of them are absolutely essential? How many are superfluous?

Time and time again, we get bombarded with television ads, supermarket, and department store catalogues that get us excited and make us drool over 50 percent to 75 percent savings on certain commodities. And so we succumb to the temptation of buying things just because they were going for half off—never mind that we don't actually need them. And they add to the clutter of an already messy house. You're familiar with DKNY (Dagdag Kalat na Naman Yan)?

So the question we should be asking ourselves when the pressure comes is, "Do I really need this item?" And every time you get a "no" answer, you will be happy. You will be happy because you have saved yourself money over a needless thing, and you have saved yourself precious space in your home.

Remember, too, that "the richest man is not he who has the most, but he who needs the least." Besides, when you get to the point that you don't have anything of these world's goods and have only God, you will still be happy because then you will find that he is all you need!

A Life That Matters

DR. JERRY BUSS, owner of the Lakers basketball organization, passed away at the age of eighty. In a program dedicated to his memory, many Laker greats like Jerry West, Magic Johnson, Shaquille O'Neal, and many more from the business and entertainment world paid tribute to his life.

He was praised not only for his business acumen and winning ways but also for his philosophy of incorporating entertainment into the world of basketball. He used his money to attract superstars with the likes of Kareem Abdul Jabbar, Magic Johnson, James Worthy, Shaquille O'Neal, Kobe Bryant, and many others. As a result, the organization has become one of the most storied and valuable franchises in the world of sports with ten world championships during his ownership. And basketball fans the world over have fun memories starting with the Showtime Lakers of the eighties to the world champion Lakers of the nineties.

I was thinking if and when our time comes to leave this world, what would people say about us? Will they pay tribute to the fact that the life we lived made a difference in the world? Will someone's life be affected so much that he will make it to heaven because of the influence of our life? The following poem written by Michael Josephson dwells on this thought.

What Will Matter

Ready or not, some day it will all come to an end.

There will be no more sunrises, no minutes, hours or days.

All the things you collected, whether treasured or forgotten, will pass to someone else.

Your wealth, fame and temporal power will shrivel to irrelevance.

It will not matter what you owned or what you were owed.

Your grudges, resentments, frustrations and jealousies will finally disappear.

So too, your hopes, ambitions, plans and to-do lists will expire.

The wins and losses that once seemed so important will fade away.

It won't matter where you came from or what side of the tracks you lived on at the end.

It won't matter whether you were beautiful or brilliant.

Even your gender and skin color will be irrelevant.

So what will matter? How will the value of your days be measured?

What will matter is not what you bought but what you built, not what you got but what you gave.

What will matter is every act of integrity, compassion, courage or sacrifice that enriched, empowered or encouraged others to emulate your example.

What will matter is not your competence but your character.

What will matter is not how many people you knew,

but how many will feel a lasting loss when you're
   gone.
What will matter is not your memories but the
   memories of those who loved you.
What will matter is how long you will be remem-
   bered, by whom and for what.
Living a life that matters doesn't happen by
   accident.
It's not a matter of circumstance but of choice.
Choose to live a life that matters.

Jesus said, "What shall it profit a man if he gains the world and lose his own soul?" (Mark 8:36).

Forgiveness and Body Weight

IN MY READING, I came across an interesting study about how the state of the mind specifically as it relates to forgiveness or grudge holding can literally have its effect on body weight and the way a person is able to carry or lift himself up.

At the Erasmus University in the Netherlands, researchers asked people to write about a time when they either gave or withheld forgiveness. They were then asked to jump as high as they could, five times, without bending their knees. Those who had forgiven the ones who wronged them jumped an average of about 11.8 inches while those who continued to hold grudges jumped 8.5 inches. The study showed that there was a huge difference in how high the two groups could jump and is a startling illustration of how forgiveness can actually unburden a person.

We sing songs about the burden of sin in our hearts being lifted at Calvary. We talk about being weighted down with the load of guilt. And how we feel so lighthearted and happy once we receive God's forgiveness and offer the same to those who have offended us. Scientific evidence is corroborating this biblical truth. It is no longer simply symbolical but is literally true.

Let us thank God for his forgiving grace, and let us be ready to offer it to those who need it from us. This brings joy to our hearts, spring in our footsteps, and the load of hatred, resentment, and bitterness off our souls.

On Bible Versions

THREE MINISTERS WERE arguing about what each considered as the best version of the Bible. One said that the King James Version was the best because it is the closest among all the Bible translations to the original languages in which the Bible was written.

The second minister expressed preference for the New International Version because it is in the language of the modern day common man. "What good is truth if it is not understood by the reader?" he asked.

The third, however, said he preferred his mother's version the best. When his two colleagues expressed surprise that his mother had her own version of the scriptures, he explained that his mom reads the Bible and then lives the truth out in her life.

And that is what Bible truth is all about. It is supposed to be read, understood, and lived out in the life so that it not only transforms the life of the reader but also serves as a powerful testimony to people within the sphere of one's influence. This was what Paul meant when he wrote to the Thessalonian believers: "[Forasmuch as ye are] manifestly declared to be the epistle of Christ ministered by us, written not with ink, but with the Spirit of the living God; not in tables of stone, but in fleshly tables of the heart" (2 Corinthians 3:3).

This is of vital importance because in a busy and materialistic world that we live in, our lives may be the only Bible that would be read by others. And so the question for us is: What kind of message do people read from the Bible of our lives?

The following poem by Arthur McPhee nails this point:

The Gospel According to You

The Gospels of Matthew, Mark, Luke, and John
Are read by more than a few,
But the one that is most read and commented on
Is the gospel according to you.

You are writing a gospel, a chapter each day
By the things that you do and the words that you say,
Men read what you write, whether faithless or true,
Say, what is the gospel according to you?

Do men read His truth and His love in your life,
Or has yours been too full of malice and strife?
Does your life speak of evil, or does it ring true?
Say, what is the gospel according to you?

May the love of Jesus and the good news of his salvation be seen and read in our lives as we live our lives each day.

Kobe's Legacy

I WAS VISITING in the home of our centenarian member who has recently been admitted to the hospital for a minor procedure. Just before I left, he asked me if I was going to watch the final game of Kobe's career in the evening, and he told me he was excited and was eagerly looking forward to watching it. I didn't have the chance to watch the game, but when I got home that night, I saw a post on Facebook by my youngest daughter, Jane, showing Nike's "Legacy" advertisement of Kobe's farewell game at Staples Center with a photo of my "preemie" grandkid Ella superimposed on it.

Surely, there is something in Kobe's dedication to the game of basketball, his work ethic, his will to win, and the skill and finesse with which he played the game that has won the hearts of millions and established his legacy across many generations. The highlights that I saw of that farewell performance were beyond impressive and a stat line of sixty points, four rebounds, and four assists is "out of this world," considering that this was the effort of a thirty-seven-year-old guy playing the last professional game of his career. Nothing could be sweeter than putting on an amazing show for the entertainment of hundreds of thousands of basketball fans while carrying one's team to victory as he rides into the sunset of his professional life.

Forget the fact that the Lakers didn't qualify for the NBA play-offs again this year and that in the last season of his career, he got stuck with a team that managed to have the worst record of wins and losses in franchise history.

As I switch mental gears however, I feel a deep sense of embarrassment as I compare superstars in the various fields of the sports and entertainment industry who go about their task with the way we do our own. So many of these successful professionals work with a passion, drive, and energy not known or seen among us. Many of us go about the king's business with such malaise, lethargy, and lackadaisical attitude as though we are content to just swim with the tide and go with the flow.

The letter of St. Paul to the Corinthians comes to us with great significance when he said, "Know ye not that they which run in a race run all, but one receives the prize? So run, that ye may obtain. And every man that strives for the mastery is temperate in all things. Now they [do it] to obtain a corruptible crown; but we an incorruptible."

Should not those of us who strive for an incorruptible crown do any less or perform less as we do God's business?

Learning from the Ants

WE HAVE BEEN admonished to go to the ant and learn from her ways. And from times past, we have known ants to be a paragon of industry and an example of good organization and provident planning for the future and the lean months ahead (Proverbs 6:6–8 and 30:24–25).

But a new study shows there's more to learn from them. And it is an encouragement to us who are growing older because what has been discovered provides us a positive outlook on the matter of aging.

Researchers at the University of Lausanne in Switzerland took an in-depth look at what goes on among carpenter ants. They tagged individual ants in six colonies with bar codes—more than six hundred worker ants total—and tracked their activity for forty-one days. A computerized camera recorded more than nine million interactions between ants that shows us how a lot of socializing goes on among these tiny creatures.

Two fascinating discoveries came up. They found out that ants divide themselves into groups based on the kind of work they do. And then as they age, they change jobs.

The young ants are nurses and caregivers. They stay close to the nest with the queen and her brood and make sure developing larvae are fed.

Middle-aged ants are the cleaners. They move trash and refuse to the garbage pile.

Older ants are foragers. They gather food for the colony, which means leaving the safety of the nest and venturing out into the world.

Foraging is the most dangerous job in the ant world. And it makes sense that the responsibility would be assumed by the oldest—and presumably wisest and most experienced—in the society of ants.

So there's the lesson for us all. We need to be contributors to society no matter what stage in life we are in. We only need to choose the ways we can involve ourselves in as we transition to a different yet no less significant role as we get older.

There's no such thing as anyone saying, "I have paid my dues. I have given my best. Let others who are younger do the job. It's time for me to take care of myself."

For as long as we are here on earth, God has a mission for us to accomplish. And we must seek to do it in order to make our lives continue to be a glory to God and a blessing to others.

And may the generations following us find us faithful and follow in our footsteps as we give back to the world the blessings of our maturity and experience.

Letter from a Parent to the Headmaster of His Son's School

FOLLOWING ARE EXCERPTS from a letter that is said to have been sent by a father to the headmaster of the school where his son was attending, the father being Abraham Lincoln.

As we go over the note, we find principles and virtues that every parent wishes to impart to a child. Needless to say, they also define the character of one who was probably the greatest president America ever had.

And if we have to learn anything, it is to transmit to our children values that will help them succeed in life as they build relationships with God and with their fellow men. Yes, we love them, but our love must be true and tough. And we need to discipline them; otherwise, we will be sparing the rod but are actually hating our child (Proverbs 13:24).

> He will have to learn, that all men are not just, all men are not true.
> But teach him also that for every scoundrel there is a hero,
> for every selfish politician, there is a dedicated leader.
>
> Teach him that for every enemy, there is a friend.
> Teach him that a dollar earned is of far more value than five found.

Teach him to learn to lose and also to enjoy
winning.
Steer him away from envy if you can.
Teach him that it is far more honorable to fail,
than to cheat.
Teach him to have faith in his own ideas,
even if everyone tells him they are wrong.
Teach him to be gentle with gentle people,
and tough with the tough.
Try to give him the strength not to follow the
crowd,
when everyone is getting on the bandwagon.
Teach him how to laugh when he is sad.
Teach him there is no shame in tears.
Teach him to close his ears to a howling mob;
and to stand and fight if he thinks he is right.
Teach him gently but do not cuddle him,
because only the test of fire makes fine steel.
Let him have the courage to be impatient,
and let him have the patience to be brave.
Teach him always to have a sublime faith in his
Creator
and faith in himself too, because then he will
always have faith in mankind.
This is a big order, but please see what you can do
for the fine little fellow, my
son.

Life Is Beautiful

OFTENTIMES, WE COMPLAIN about our situation in life. We whine, and we pout because things are not what we want them to be. But when we realize that things could really be worse, we can choose to "grin and bear it."

In Budapest, a man goes to the rabbi and complains, "Life is unbearable. There are nine of us living in one room. What can I do?"

The rabbi answers, "Take your goat into the room with you." The man is incredulous, but the rabbi insists. "Do as I say and come back in a week."

A week later, the man comes back, looking more distraught than before. "We cannot stand it," he tells the rabbi. "The goat is filthy."

The rabbi then tells him, "Go home and let the goat out. And come back in a week."

A radiant man returns to the rabbi a week later, exclaiming, "Life is beautiful. We enjoy every minute of it now that there's no goat, only the nine of us."

There was no numerical change of the man's family from the before-and-after scenarios. There were nine of them to start with. And they were miserable. There were also nine of them at the end. But they were a happy bunch. The only difference was the fact that at the conclusion of the story, they got rid of a problem that they didn't have initially.

The apostle Paul says, "I have learned in whatever state I am to be content" (Philippians 4:11).

The Difference of One

MANY TIMES, WE don't take action because we think our contribution is so insignificant it won't make any waves in the ocean of life. So we end up doing nothing, and our world is deprived of the good we would have done.

But just think for a moment if you went ahead and did it anyway. You can affect one life and that life, in turn, could touch another for good, and before long, the world has become a better place. So don't even think about it. Just do it, and your good will multiply for the blessing of humanity.

The following poem written by an anonymous author highlights this point:

> One song can spark a moment,
> One flower can wake the dream
> One tree can start a forest,
> One bird can herald spring.
>
> One smile begins a friendship,
> One handclasp lifts a soul.
> One star can guide a ship at sea,
> One word can frame the goal
>
> One vote can change a nation,
> One sunbeam lights a room

One candle wipes out darkness,
One laugh will conquer gloom.

One step must start each journey.
One word must start each prayer.
One hope will raise our spirits,
One touch can show you care.

One voice can speak with wisdom,
One heart can know what's true,
One life can make a difference,
You see, it's up to you!

So go ahead, light your candle, and from your corner, watch the darkness flee away as it gives way to a world of light.

Positive Living in a Negative World

WHEN WE BANISH negativism in our lives and commit to positive thoughts and ideas, we become better able to face life's realities in whatever form they take. So never panic or give up. More often than not, problems have a way of solving themselves, or you get surprised with something that opens up that you never imagined before.

So as soon as you get up in the morning, set your mind into gear for the day. Say to yourself the following:

- Today is going to be a great day.
- I can handle more than I think I can.
- Things don't get better by worrying about them.
- I can be satisfied if I try to do my best.
- There is always something to be happy about.
- I'm going to make someone happy today.
- It's not good to be down.
- Life is great. Make the most of it.

We don't have to fake it because we have everything on our side. This was what the prophet Habakkuk meant when he wrote in his book (chapter 3:17–18):

> Though the fig tree may not blossom, nor fruit
> be on the vines;
> Though the labor of the olive may fail, and the
> fields yield no food;

Though the flock may be cut off from the fold,
And there be no herd in the stalls—
Yet I will rejoice in the Lord, I will joy in the God
of my Salvation.

However dark the circumstances and no matter how grim the situation may be, the outlook will still be positive, and we can still rejoice because Christ has given us salvation by his death, and we can still be happy because eternal life is ours.

Making Friends for Health and Long Life

LEONARD SYME, A professor of epidemiology at the University of California at Berkeley, indicates the importance of social ties and social support systems in relationship to disease rates and mortality.

He points to Japan as being the number one nation in the world with respect to health and then discusses the close social, cultural, and traditional ties in that country as the reason. He believes that the more social ties, the better the health and the lower the death rate. Conversely, he says that the more isolated the person, the poorer the health and the higher the death rate.

Social ties such as friendships and family relationships are good preventative medicine for physical and mental-emotional-behavior problems.

So let us start making friends and make sure these friends are the kind that are true and genuine, not the fake and plastic ones. And to succeed at this, we need to first be a friend. The Bible says, "A man that has friends must himself be friendly. But there is a friend that sticks closer than a brother" (Proverbs 18:24).

In his farewell conversation with his disciples, Jesus told them that he elevated their status from servants to that of friends. And I believe it is because Jesus loves us so much he wants us to enjoy life and live long for his glory by maintaining a friendship with him. In fact, friendship with Jesus improves the quality and quantity of our years here on earth. It even guarantees eternal life in heaven and on the earth made new.

You may not be intentionally aiming for it but making and keeping really good friends is one secret to a healthier and longer lasting you! And making and keeping our friendship with Jesus gives us total satisfaction here in this life and an eternity in our heavenly home.

Who Will Tell Them?

I ATTENDED THE last meeting for all Health Information Centers for the Pathway to Health-Los Angeles at the White Memorial Church for final instructions before the mega clinic at the Los Angeles Convention Center began. Toward the end, the event coordinator called attention to the stack of flyers and invitations sitting on the front pews. She reminded us all that every flyer represented a soul who was a candidate for the kingdom and appealed that everyone get a bunch of these invitations to give away to whoever would receive them before they left.

I picked up a couple hundred flyers and went downtown where the homeless people camp out. I covered the area of San Pedro Street that is crossed by Fifth, Sixth, and Seventh Streets. This is where those that are down and out on their luck live, close to where Union Rescue Mission and the Midnight Mission are located and where they give away food.

I gave away the flyers. I visited and talked with them. A few had stories to tell. Many were excited to have the chance for the free services while some didn't care as they said they were covered and a few others claimed they had their own personal physicians.

I will never know how many of those who received the invitations showed up at the convention center. But some of the lab results indicate that certain of them do not have addresses as they live on the city streets.

The point I wish to emphasize is that there are people around us who are poor and needy, and we need to go and do what we can to help them. We can't choose who to go to. In fact, we should even focus our efforts on the less fortunate members of society, the have-nots, and the marginalized. These are the special objects of Christ's mission and ministry.

And he wants us to do his work for them. For if we don't go, who will. And if we don't share the good news of the kingdom with them, how will they ever know?

Hang On

SUCCESS AND HAPPINESS in life depend on the achievement of our goals. And the goals we set have to be based on what we believe to be the purpose of our life here on earth.

The questions we need to be asking are: Do we know why we are here on earth? Are our goals set in harmony with this purpose in life? Do we live every day so that each day brings us closer to our goals.

And if we find ourselves so far removed from where we ought to be and get discouraged that we may not even get there, let's not give up. Keep going on. The road may be rough, and storms may threaten our progress. But if we know where we are going, we just have to move on no matter how slow our pace may be. Determination, guts, and courage will help us get there.

There is a poem that inspires the beleaguered pilgrim along life's way:

Keep Going On

Keep going on,
even if the darkness
envelops you totally;
for light shall come soon,
to light up the way.

Keep going on,
even if the waves roar
at your very feet;
for calm will come,
and the waves will recede.

Keep going on,
even if you feel totally worn out.
The fruit you will get
will be unimaginably sweet.
Keep going on.

And when you believe that God will be your helper and guide, there's no doubt you are going to make it. Paul says in Philippians 1:6, "Being confident of this very thing, that He who has begun a good work in you will complete it until the day of Jesus Christ."

True Friendship

LOVE AND FRIENDSHIP are special blessings, and it is good to thank the Lord for them. These gifts enrich and bring fulfillment to our lives. Without love and friends, life would be without joy and meaning. Think how your life would be without these joys.

Michael Josephson defines what friends are with all the letters of the alphabet. Think about each of the following statements.

True Friendship A–Z

Accepts you as you are	Never abandons you
Believes in you	Opens doors for you
Celebrates your successes	Prods you
Defends you	Quells your fears
Encourages you	Restores your confidence
Forgives you no matter what	Shares your joys and grief
Gives you what you need	Tells you the truth
Has patience with you	Understands you best
Inspires you	Values you
Judges you rarely but fairly	Wants the best for you
Keeps your secrets	Xpects the best from you
Loves you for who you are	Yanks you back to reality
Makes you feel better	Zeros in on what's wrong

We need to cultivate our friendships not only for what friends and loved ones can do for us but also by being the true friend that we can be to them, especially to those who are in need of our love and friendship.

And remember, we have a friend who sticks closer than a brother (Proverbs 18:24). And he wants us to be his forever friend.

God's Word Not to Return Void

ONE OF THE five non-Seventh-day Adventists who joined us in our Bible Prophecy and Reformation Tour of Central and Eastern Europe is a Roman Catholic. She is a retired nurse from Riverside who has come along with her family in previous trips. Obviously, she has enjoyed traveling with our groups before, and this time, she again came along, together with two of her teenaged grandkids.

I felt a little awkward and uncomfortable every time we stopped at the Reformation sites and read portions of the book, *The Great Controversy*. In fact, I wondered a few times during the tour if she was regretting joining this trip or if she thought her European "vacation" was being ruined by our constant references to the pope and the Roman Catholic Church persecuting God's faithful people during the 1,260 years of papal supremacy. I wondered what she thought when we visited the sites of the martyrdom of Huss and Jerome, the Waldensian Valleys and caves where "the true church" went into hiding from the armies of the papacy, the place where Martin Luther made a stand against the pressure to recant and retract his teachings against the church of Rome, the St. Bartholomew's Massacre in Paris, France by instigation of the papacy.

On the last day of our tour, while doing a leisurely sightseeing in the city of Prague, I finally asked what she thought of the whole experience. She responded that she enjoyed it so much and told me that she was especially grateful that her two grandkids got exposed to our teachings and given a large dose of "religion" because she said they didn't go to church. And then she asked, "By the way, can I keep your book?" referring to *The Great Controversy* that I gave at the beginning of our trip as a reference for our studies.

Another non-SDA who joined us is a nurse from Moreno Valley who currently attends a Protestant Church. She sent a card soon after our arrival, expressing profuse gratitude for the experience of a lifetime she had during the tour—mentioning not only the privilege of seeing so many beautiful sceneries in the many countries visited but also being with such a wonderful group of people and the opportunity to learn about Church Reformation history. She also was grateful for *The Great Controversy* volume that she has now in her possession.

Eternity alone will tell how many will get to heaven as a result of the books and literature that have been shared with them. Renato Daluyen, Dean and Celly Jane Mercurio, Ellie Wong, and others in the group came on tour, loaded with glow tracts to share with anyone who might be willing to receive. From Rome (Italy) to Paris (France), at Budapest (Hungary) and then at Vienna (Austria) and finally Prague in the Czech Republic, literature was distributed and who can tell how many will get to the kingdom of heaven from those contacts?

The scriptures declare, "For as the rain cometh down, and the snow from heaven, and returneth not thither, but watereth the earth, and maketh it bring forth and bud, that it may give seed to the sower, and bread to the eater: so shall my word be that goeth forth out of my mouth: it shall not return unto me void, but it shall accomplish that which I please and it shall prosper in the thing whereto I sent it" (Isaiah 55:10 –11).

Only Jesus Saves

A SOLDIER IN Napoleon's army was mortally wounded in battle. As the last struggle drew near and he lay dying in his tent, he sent for his chief. Napoleon came.

The poor man thought his emperor could do anything. So he earnestly pleaded with him to save his life. The emperor sadly shook his head and turned away.

And as the cold, merciless hand of death drew him irresistibly behind the curtain of the unseen world, the man was heard to continue to press his plea, "Save me, Napoleon! Save me!"

In the hour of death, that soldier discovered that even the powerful Napoleon could not give him life. But we have someone who not only can save us and heal us from our physical infirmities. He is able to redeem us from sin and death by his death on the cross of Calvary. He paid the penalty for our sins and now offers us the gift of eternal life.

Before Jesus ascended to heaven, he instituted the rite of communion, and every time we partake of the bread and the wine that are emblems of his broken body and spilled blood, we are to remember what he did to save us. He said, "Do this in remembrance of Me" (1 Corinthians 11:24–25).

And of course, we are to remember him not only during the celebration of the Lord's Supper. We are to remember him and his sacrificial death every day of our lives until he comes again to take all his children home.

Parable of the Frogs

A GROUP OF frogs was traveling through the woods, and two of them fell into a deep pit. All the other frogs gathered around the pit. When they saw how deep the pit was, they told the two frogs that it was impossible for them to get out and that they were as good as dead.

The two frogs, however, ignored the comments and tried to jump out of the pit with all of their might.

The other frogs kept telling them to stop that it was no use for them to keep on jumping and that they were as good as dead.

Finally, one of the frogs took heed to what the other frogs were saying and gave up. He dropped down and died.

The other frog continued to jump as hard as he could. Once again, the crowd of frogs yelled at him to quit trying and just die. He jumped even harder and finally made it out.

Once out, the other frogs said, "Did you not hear us?"

The frog explained to them that he was deaf. He actually thought that they were encouraging him the whole time.

This simple story shows us that there is power in the tongue. Words spoken can spell the difference between life and death. They can be a blessing, and they can also be a curse.

An encouraging word to someone who is down can lift him up and help him make it through the day.

On the other hand, a destructive word to someone who is down can be what it takes to kill him or her.

The apostle James says, "Out of the same mouth proceed blessing and cursing. My brethren, these things ought not to be so" (3:10).

Let us be careful then with the words we speak. Let us speak life to those who happen to cross our paths. It may well be God has placed them there so they can get encouragement from us. Let our words lift them up and push them forward past the obstacles and barriers in their journey and guide them safely through to their final destination.

Puppies for Sale

A STORE OWNER was tacking a sign above his door that read "Puppies for Sale." Signs like that have a way of attracting small children, and sure enough, a little boy appeared under the store owner's sign. "How much are you going to sell the puppies for?" he asked.

The store owner replied, "Anywhere from $30 to $50."

The little boy reached in his pocket and pulled out some change. "I have $2.37," he said. "Can I please look at them?"

The store owner smiled and whistled and out of the kennel came lady, who ran down the aisle of his store followed by five teeny, tiny balls of fur.

One puppy was lagging considerably behind. Immediately, the little boy singled out the lagging, limping puppy and said, "What's wrong with that little dog?"

The store owner explained that the veterinarian had examined the little puppy and had discovered it didn't have a hip socket. It would always limp. It would always be lame.

The little boy became excited. "That is the puppy that I want to buy."

The store owner said, "No, you don't want to buy that little dog. If you really want him, I'll just give him to you."

The little boy got quite upset. He looked straight into the store owner's eyes, pointing his finger and said, "I don't want you to give him to me. That little dog is worth every bit as much as all the other dogs, and I'll pay full price. In fact, I'll give you $2.37 now and 50¢ a month until I have him paid for."

The store owner countered, "You really don't want to buy this little dog. He is never going to be able to run and jump and play with you like the other puppies."

The little boy reached down and rolled up his pant leg to reveal a badly twisted, crippled left leg supported by a big metal brace. He looked up at the store owner and softly replied, "Well, I don't run so well myself, and the little puppy will need someone who understands!"

Was this not why Jesus became like one of us and was in all points tempted so that he is able to help those of us that are tempted?

Hebrews 2:17–18 says, "Wherefore in all things it behoved him to be made like unto [his] brethren, that he might be a merciful and faithful high priest in things [pertaining] to God, to make reconciliation for the sins of the people. For in that he himself hath suffered being tempted, he is able to succour them that are tempted."

Let us come to him who is willing and able to help us. He is our merciful and faithful high priest.

The Quest for Happiness

A GROUP OF people was attending a seminar. In the middle of the presentation, the speaker stopped and decided to do a group activity. He began by giving each one a balloon. Each was to write his name on it using a marker pen. Then the balloons were collected and put in another room.

The participants were then let in that room and were asked to find the balloon that had their name written on it within five minutes. Soon everyone was frantically searching for his name, bumping into each other, and pushing others around. The place was turned into utter chaos.

After five minutes, no one has found his own balloon.

The speaker then gave a different set of instructions. Each one was asked to randomly collect a balloon and give it to the person who had his name on it.

Within minutes, everyone had his own balloon.

The speaker then said, "What happened here is exactly what is happening in our lives. Everyone is frantically looking for his own happiness, not knowing where it is."

But happiness lies not in seeking our own pleasure. It is found in the very act of serving and ministering to the needs of others. Give happiness to others, and happiness will come to you. Spread sunshine, and you will find yourself removed from the shades of night.

This is what life on earth is all about. This was why Jesus Christ left heaven to come to this world. He says, "For even the Son of Man did not come to be served, but to serve and to give his life a ransom for many" (Mark 10:45).

Shake Off Your Problems

A STORY IS told about a farmer's donkey that fell into a dry well. The man tried to pull it out, but he couldn't no matter how hard he tried. Thinking that there was no other way to get it out and considering that the donkey was already old and its best years behind it, the farmer decided to bury it alive and let it go to its rest.

So the farmer started pouring soil into the donkey's back. But as the donkey feels the dirt, it shakes it off and steps on it. More soil is poured. And each time, the donkey shakes it off and steps up. And the more the load was poured, the higher it rose. By noon, the donkey was grazing in green pastures.

Just a little story to encourage us that we should never be discouraged by the burdens and trials that life hurls upon us. We should not allow problems to bury us and destroy our usefulness. Make these obstacles stepping-stones to greater heights of success and happiness. If you don't lose hope like the old donkey, you will soon be stepping up and out into freedom and before long you will find yourselves grazing in green pastures.

And if a donkey can do this, you sure could do it and could do it even better! The apostle James says (1:3–4), "Knowing this, that the trying of your faith works patience. But let patience have her perfect work, that ye may be perfect and entire, wanting nothing."

Something Big Is Coming

SOMETIMES, PEOPLE GET discouraged and give up when they find themselves "down and out on their luck." But in a lot of cases, that is when they are about to achieve success, and so they miss out big time. They learn too late that a quitter never wins, and a winner never quits.

So when you find yourself out in the dumps, do not quit. Instead, get yourself ready and primed up for something big that could happen in your life. Consider the arrow.

Someone observed:

> An arrow can only be shot by pulling it backward.
> So when life is dragging you back with difficulties,
> It means that it's going to launch you into something great.

Instead of giving up, prepare to be launched out into something great. That's what happened with Moses after spending forty years in obscurity in the wilderness of Midian or with Paul for three years in the desert of Arabia or with Joseph for several years in a dark and dreary dungeon in Egypt. They hung on and persevered. They waited on God's faithfulness, and their faith got rewarded.

Something big is coming. And you better be ready for it.

A Story of Success

ONE DAY, THOMAS Edison came home and gave a paper to his mother. He told her, "My teacher gave this paper to me and told me to only give it to my mother."

His mother's eyes were tearful as she read the letter out loud to her child, "Your son is a genius. This school is too small for him and doesn't have enough good teachers for training him. Please teach him yourself."

After many, many years following Edison's mother's death, and he was now one of the greatest inventors of the century, he was looking through some old family things one day. His eyes fell on a folded paper in the corner of a drawer in a desk. He took it and opened it up.

On the paper was written, "Your son is addled [mentally ill]. We won't let him come to school anymore."

Edison cried for hours, and then he wrote in his diary, "Thomas Alva Edison was an addled child that, by a hero mother, became the genius of the century."

Some people do not see the "diamond in the rough" or the limitless potential in others like Thomas Edison's teacher. But thank God for moms like Edison's who have faith in others and won't give up in the face of adversity. Think of what blessings our world would have been deprived of if Edison's mom believed the prejudiced evaluation of her son's teacher and gave up on her child.

The fact is, we all have potential because we have been made in the image of God. Let us not give up on ourselves or on others. Let us develop the gift God gave to us and let us strive to be a blessing to the world.

Profile of a Strong Family

IN A NATIONAL survey of strong families conducted by the Human Development and Family Department at the University of Nebraska-Lincoln (1983), the following profile of a strong family was created:

1. Appreciation. "Family members gave one another compliments and sincere demonstrations of approval. They tried to make the others feel appreciated and good about themselves."

2. Ability to Deal with Crises in a Positive Manner. "They were willing to take a bad situation, see something positive in it and focus on that."

3. Time Together. "In all areas of their lives—meals, work, recreation—they structured their schedules to spend time together."

4. High Degree of Commitment. "Families promoted each person's happiness and welfare, invested time and energy in each other, and made family their number one priority."

5. Good Communication Patterns. "These families spent time talking with each other. They also listened well, which shows respect."

6. High Degree of Religious Orientation. "Not all belonged to an organized church, but they considered themselves highly religious."

It just surprises me that genuine, unconditional love is not among the above listed qualities. Or could it have been simply assumed? Anyway, I believe love is the glue that holds any relationship together if it is to be an enjoyable and lasting one. And this is true whether we are talking about our biological family, our family in the workplace, or our church family. Jesus said to his disciples, "By this shall all men know that you are My disciples if you have love for one another" (John 13:35).

Finally, as we look at the strong family profile once again, let us rate ourselves. Are our families strong or are they weak? If they are strong, we can make them even stronger. And if they are weak, we can make them strong.

Ten Quotes to Jump-Start Your Day

FOLLOWING ARE SOME inspirational quotes that can help jump-start our day. They can help us deal with the obstacles and challenges we face, work out our relationships, and even create an attitude that can make us move past the negativity that oftentimes surround us.

1. No matter how good or bad you think life is, wake up each day and be thankful for life. Someone somewhere else is fighting to survive.
2. Appreciate, cherish, and be grateful.
3. Fake people hate honesty. It's the lies that keep them feeling good about themselves and their lives. So share your true feelings about their actions and watch how they fade away.
4. Don't let anyone's ignorance, hate, drama, or negativity stop you from being the best person you can be.
5. A smart person will give you smart answers, but a wise person will ask you smart questions.
6. Never chase love, affection, or attention. If it isn't given freely by another person, it isn't worth having.
7. Coming together is a beginning. Keeping together is progress. Working together is success.
8. Don't confuse your path with your destination. Just because it's stormy now doesn't mean that you aren't headed for sunshine.

9. Obstacles can't stop you; problems can't stop you; most of all, other people can't stop you. The only one who can really stop you is yourself.
10. The way you treat yourself sets the standard for others on how you demand to be treated. Don't settle for anything other than respect.

So be grateful for each day. God graciously gives it to you as a gift. Show gratitude by enjoying it to the fullest and using each moment to glorify his name and bless others.

Be Thankful for Your Troubles

IN THE UNITED States, Thanksgiving is officially celebrated once a year, and when the season comes, it is a great time to remember God's blessings in a special way and count them one by one. As we do this, we will be surprised "to see what God has done."

The scriptures, however, urge us not to just be thankful for life's blessings. We are to thank God even for our troubles and our sorrows. In Ephesians 5:19, Paul writes, "Giving thanks always for all things unto God and the Father in the name of our Lord Jesus Christ." This may be difficult to do for how can we be thankful for all things, which could include our disappointments, our trials, and our tears?

The following poem shows us how this can be possible, and reading it gives us light on the words of the apostle.

> Be thankful that you don't already have everything you desire.
>> If you did, what would there be to look forward to?
> Be thankful when you don't know something,
>> for it gives you the opportunity to learn.
>
> Be thankful for the difficult times.
>> During those times you grow.
> Be thankful for your limitations,

because they give you opportunities for
improvement.
Be thankful for each new challenge,
    because it will build your strength and
    character.

Be thankful for your mistakes.
    They will teach you valuable lessons.
Be thankful when you're tired and weary,
    because it means you've made a difference.

It's easy to be thankful for the good things.
    A life of rich fulfillment comes to those who
    are also thankful for the setbacks.
Gratitude can turn a negative into a positive.
    Find a way to be thankful for your troubles,
    and they can become your blessings.

So let us do as the Word of God says. Let us *give thanks always*
for *all things* unto God in the name of our Lord Jesus Christ. We need
to do this for this is "the will of God" for our lives (1 Thessalonians
5:18).

The Amazing Powers of the Mind

IN *THE ANATOMY of an Illness: As Perceived by the Patient,* Norman Cousins tells of being hospitalized with a rare, crippling disease. When he was diagnosed as incurable, Cousins checked out of the hospital. Aware of the harmful effects that negative emotions can have on the body, Cousins reasoned the reverse was true. So he borrowed a movie projector and prescribed his own treatment, consisting of Marx Brothers films and old *Candid Camera* reruns.

It didn't take long for him to discover that ten minutes of laughter provided two hours of pain-free sleep. Amazingly, his debilitating disease was eventually reversed. After the account of his victory appeared in the *New England Journal of Medicine,* Cousins received more than three thousand letters from appreciative physicians throughout the world.

Today we talk about psychosomatic diseases. Because of the close relationship between the mind and the body, what affects the mind affects the body, and what affects the body affects the mind. Psychosomatic disorders are illnesses that are caused by the condition of the mind.

Cousins's documented experience and from what we already know about physical science and medicine should make us determine to discipline our minds and train them to dwell on sublime and happy thoughts in order to maintain a healthy body. We are not to dwell on any negative thoughts or allow our minds to be trapped with unpleasant and ugly things that will only pull us down. Let us think heavenly thoughts and stay only with the positive experiences of life.

Paul has this to say, "Finally brethren, whatsoever things are true, whatsoever things are honest, whatsoever things are just, whatsoever things are pure, whatsoever things are lovely, whatsoever things are of good report; if there is any virtue and if there is any praise, think on these things" (Philippians 4:8).

Truth in Its Fullness

ONCE THE DEVIL was walking along with one of his cohorts. They saw a man ahead of them pick up something shiny.

"What did he find?" asked the cohort.

"A piece of the truth," the devil replied.

"Doesn't it bother you that he found a piece of the truth?" asked the cohort.

"No," said the devil, "I will see to it that he makes a religion out of it."

In our spiritual journey, we oftentimes pick up truth and rejoice at what we have discovered through the outworking of the Holy Spirit.

The enemy of our souls, however, would not give up that easily. He may not try to wrest the truth away. He would just try to make us think that, that is all the truth there is. And then we spend a lifetime working and talking about what we have discovered as though that is the only gospel there is in this whole wide world.

Truth, by its very nature, is mysterious. It is unfathomable and infinite. What we see and discover may just be a facet that is an invitation to probe deeper in order to behold the truth in all its glory and resplendence.

So let us learn to view truth the way it should be. Let us look at the total picture. And in our sharing and teaching, let people have the truth in its entirety. Jesus would say, "These you ought to have done without leaving the others undone" (Matthew 23:23). And Paul would later say in Acts 20:27, "For I have not shunned to declare unto you the WHOLE counsel of God."

Let us not allow the devil to have us make a religion of what we have found. Because there are a host of other aspects of truth that are part of God's gracious revelation to us.

The Elephant Rope

As a man was walking in the park, he saw some elephants, and he stopped, confused by the fact that these huge creatures were being held by only a small rope tied to their front leg. There were no chains or cages to hold them in. It was obvious that the elephants could at any time break away from their bonds, but for some reason, they did not.

He saw a trainer nearby and asked why these animals just stood there and made no attempt to get away.

"Well," the trainer said, "when they are very young and much smaller, we use the same size rope to tie them, and at that age, it's enough to hold them. As they grow up, they are conditioned to believe they cannot break away. They believe the rope can still hold them, so they never try to break free."

The man was amazed. These animals could at any time break free from their bonds, but because they believed they couldn't, they were stuck right where they were.

Like the elephants, how many of us go through life hanging onto a belief that we cannot do something simply because we failed at it once before?

This story highlights the power of the mind. If you think you can, you can. And if you think you can't, you surely can't. So give yourself the benefit of the doubt. Someone said, "Whatever the human mind can believe, it can achieve."

Break through your worries and fears. And never mind that some people will tell you, you can't do it because of your background or your training or because of anything you may not possess. Think of the bumblebee, which according to experts on the laws of aerodynamics, could not fly because of its morphology. Its wings are too small compared to the size and bulk of its body. But it doesn't know that, and it tries to fly anyway, and before you know it, it's up soaring in the sky.

In the spiritual life, it is the same. There is power available for you, and it is all yours for the asking. Go through life with an attitude of victory over bad habits and formidable challenges.

As Paul has said, "I can do all things through Christ who strengthens me" (Philippians 4:13).

A Successful Mission Outreach

As WE TAXIED down the runway at Los Angeles International Airport, coming home from a successful mission trip to the Philippines, the bright lights of the city afforded us a welcome sight. And even as we drove down the freeway, across downtown and to the residential districts of Eagle Rock, Sunland, and Lake View Terrace, I felt a special calm in mind and spirit. This was all too different from the chaotic conditions that we've been through, i.e., the traffic situation in Manila, Cagayan de Oro, and Cebu, and the hectic and packed schedules that we maintained the last two weeks.

But all went well with the medical mission and the evangelistic outreach. There were 90 baptized at the end of the series of meetings. This brings the total to 225 already baptized for our church outreach project including the 135 baptized prior to our arrival. And since our budget allows for one more month for the five lay preachers to be doing follow-up work, there should be a lot more added to this number. Praise be to God for his marvelous work in the hearts of men!

As we praise God for his guidance through the Holy Spirit and thank him for his watch care over us, we extend a heartfelt appreciation to all of you who gave support to the project with your means, and for all the prayers you have offered for our safe return.

May his rich blessings rest upon us as we once again take up the work he has committed to us here.

The Little Difference That Makes a Big Difference

PEOPLE ARE BASICALLY the same. In spite of our many differences, we still share the same elemental needs, hopes, and dreams. Every day that we live is powered by the desire to improve our lot and achieve our goal of being able to live in peace, comfort, and happiness. W. Clement Stone once said, "There is little difference in people, but that little difference makes a big difference. The little difference is attitude. The big difference is whether it is positive or negative."

In the following poem entitled "The Optimist Creed" written by Christian Larson, he urges that we focus only on the positive, the best, and the sunny side of life. This expands on what Stone has said in terms of the little difference that makes a big difference in people's lives.

Promise Yourself

To be so strong that nothing can disturb your
    peace of mind.
To talk health, happiness and prosperity to every
    person you meet.
To make all your friends feel that there is some-
    thing in them.
To look at the sunny side of everything and make
    your optimism come true.

To think only of the best, to work only for the
best and to expect only the best.

To be just as enthusiastic about the success of
others as you are about your own.

To forget the mistakes of the past and press on to
the greater achievements of the future.

To wear a cheerful countenance at all times and
give every living creature you meet a smile.

To give so much time to the improvement of
yourself that you have no time to criticize
others.

To be too large for worry, too noble for anger, too
strong for fear, and too happy to permit the
presence of trouble.

And this was how Jesus our Lord "endured the cross, despising the shame" because he focused on the "joy that was set before him" (Hebrews 12:2).

And it's the same principle Paul suggests that we go by to succeed in our spiritual lives. We "do not look at the things that are seen but at the things which are not seen. For the things that are seen are temporary, but the things that are not seen are eternal" (2 Corinthians 4:18).

The Power Behind Our Words

A WOMAN ONCE came to Gandhi and asked him to please tell her son to give up eating sugar. Gandhi asked the woman to bring the boy back in a week. Exactly one week later, the woman returned, and Gandhi said to the boy, "Please give up eating sugar."

The woman thanked Gandhi, and as she turned to go, she asked him why he had not said those words a week before to which the Mahatma replied, "Because a week ago, I had not given up eating sugar."

Gandhi would be later known to have said the words, "You must be the change you wish to see in the world."

As change agents, we need to realize that the power of our words find their source from the power of our lives. That is why there was power in the words of Jesus. On one occasion when the police officers were sent to arrest him and came back empty handed, they were asked by the authorities why they haven't brought him. And their simple response was "No man ever spoke like this Man!" (John 7:46).

My professor at the Seventh-day Adventist Theological Seminary Dr. Norman Gulley would tell our class that the reason Jesus spoke like no other man was because he lived like no other man. His life that was lived in the truth was the source of power behind those words.

So if we want to see change in our families, our neighborhoods, our churches, and our world, let the change begin in us. Let us live out the principles of truth in our lives, and then our words will carry the force that God can use to change the world.

Things Happen for a Reason

I WAS AT the doctor's office one day for a routine checkup, and I had to wait exceptionally longer than usual. After about two hours, the doctor came, and he was very apologetic. He explained that the computers were down and that's how the schedules got messed up. Technology that has been a tremendous boon to society can be crippling and disruptive at times.

But I really didn't mind because I read and got busy the whole time. I had my tablet with me, and so I actually welcomed the large chunk of time that became available for some moments of thinking and meditation.

I came across a material with some sage advice for happiness in life. It goes this way:

1. Life is too short to be anything but happy.
2. Love deeply.
3. Forgive quickly.
4. Take chances.
5. Give everything with no regrets.
6. Forget the past with the exception of what you have learned.
7. Remember everything happens for a reason.

Each one of these thoughts is a sound principle to live by and the last one in particular is almost a quote from the apostle Paul. It's true that things happen for a reason, and it's for a good reason for those who are God's faithful children. This encourages us to look for the positive in every circumstance in life, no matter how badly things may seem to appear.

Romans 8:28 says, "And we know that all things work together for good to those who love God, to them who are the called according to His purpose."

The Three Trees

Once there were three trees on a hill in the woods. They were discussing their hopes and dreams when the first tree said, "Someday I hope to be a treasure chest. I could be filled with gold, silver, and precious gems. I could be decorated with intricate carving, and everyone would see the beauty."

Then the second tree said, "Someday I will be a mighty ship. I will take kings and queens across the waters and sail to the corners of the world. Everyone will feel safe in me because of the strength of my hull."

Finally, the third tree said, "I want to grow to be the tallest and straightest tree in the forest. People will see me on top of the hill and look up to my branches, and think of the heavens and God and how close to them I am reaching. I will be the greatest tree of all time, and people will always remember me."

After a few years of praying that their dreams would come true, a group of woodsmen came upon the trees. When one came to the first tree, he said, "This looks like a strong tree. I think I should be able to sell the wood to a carpenter." And he began cutting it down. The tree was happy because he knew that the carpenter would make him into a treasure chest.

At the second tree, the woodsman said, "This looks like a strong tree. I should be able to sell it to the shipyard." The second tree was happy because he knew he was on his way to becoming a mighty ship.

When the woodsmen came upon the third tree, the tree was frightened because he knew that if they cut him down, his dreams would not come true. One of the woodsmen said, "I don't need anything special from my tree. I'll take this one." And he cut it down.

When the first tree arrived at the carpenter's, he was made into a feed box for animals. He was then placed in a barn and filled with hay. This was not at all what he had prayed for.

The second tree was cut and made into a small fishing boat. His dreams of being a mighty ship and carrying kings had come to an end.

The third tree was cut into large pieces and left alone in the dark.

The years went by, and the trees forgot about their dreams. Then one day, a man and woman came to the barn. She gave birth, and they placed the baby in the hay in the feed box that was made from the first tree. The man wished that he could have made a crib for the baby, but this manger would have to do. The tree could feel the importance of this event and knew that it had held the greatest treasure of all time.

Years later, a group of men got in the fishing boat made from the second tree. One of them was tired and went to sleep. While they were out on the water, a great storm arose, and the tree didn't think it was strong enough to keep the men safe. The men woke the sleeping man, and he stood and said, "Peace," and the storm stopped. At this time, the tree knew that it had carried the king of kings in its boat.

Finally, someone came and got the third tree. It was carried through the streets as the people mocked the man who was carrying it. When they came to a stop, the man was nailed to the tree and raised in the air to die at the top of a hill. The tree came to realize that it was strong enough to stand at the top of the hill and be as close to God as was possible because Jesus had been crucified on it.

This story tells us that when things don't seem to be going our way, we need to know that God has a plan for us. If we place our trust in him, he will give us our heart's desires. Each of the trees got what they wanted, just not in the way they had imagined. We don't always know what God's plans are for us. We just know that his ways are not our ways, but his ways are always best.

Who Do You Look Like?

ON A WALL near the main entrance to the Alamo in San Antonio, Texas, is a portrait with the following inscription, "James Butler Bonham—no picture of him exists. This portrait is of his nephew, Major James Bonham, deceased, who greatly resembled his uncle. It is placed here by the family that people may know the appearance of the man who died for freedom."

An old Bible that I used to own had some interesting Bible trivia as a supplemental material in it. One of them was a page that gave a purported description of Jesus Christ. Of course, we know there is no existing literal portrait of him.

However, it is the goal of each one of us to be like Jesus (not so much in the physical aspects of his person but) in spirit and in his character. And the good thing about that is that we don't have to worry about how this could be done because the Holy Spirit has promised to make this happen for us.

The apostle Paul declares, "But we all, with open face beholding as in a glass the glory of the Lord, are changed into the same image from glory to glory, [even] as by the Spirit of the Lord" (2 Corinthians 3:18).

And E. G. White says in her book *Christ's Object Lessons*, p. 69, "When the character of Christ has been perfectly reproduced in His people, He will come and claim them as His own."

Do we almost look like him now? Are we about ready to go home?

Trees of God's Planting

THE FALL SEASON was coming to a close, and I was in our backyard looking at a sizeable inclined space that stretched to the end of our property. It wasn't a pretty sight. Twenty-five years ago when we first occupied the place, the area was planted with ornamental shrubs and greenery. Through neglect, it was now overgrown with weeds.

I decided to transform the place and bring it back to its original beauty, if not into an even more pleasant place than it was before. I was going to plant fruit trees where now there are only weeds.

It was a tall order. But I was willing to take the challenge upon myself. First, I cleared the place of all unwanted weeds. Then I had to use some engineering skills to carve steps and walkways on the steep and hilly surface. Then I had to dig holes where I wanted the trees. This was the toughest part of the project as the ground was almost rock-solid and oftentimes I had to pour water and soak the soil overnight for me to go deeper.

Finally, the work was done, and as I looked at the twenty-two fruit trees on the hill where before there were only weeds, I was glad. In fact, I looked twelve months ahead for the first season, and I could see in my mind's eye a wonderful assortment of pomegranates, lemons, oranges, peaches, nectarines, apricots, avocados, mangoes, and sapote.

But then came winter, and the cold and the chill threatened my hopes and dreams. Except for the citrus trees, all the rest shed off their leaves, and I wondered if they would survive their first winter in their new environment.

Spring came, however, with its warm and balmy weather. And even in the first few days, I began to see new leaves shooting forth. And a few of them began breaking out with flowers and buds. I only hope they would be stable enough to sustain their blossoms and that these would turn into fruit to compensate for my labor.

One mango tree didn't survive. The chilly winds of the winter months were just too much, and it died. Not bad on a percentage basis as far as survival was concerned.

This experience has taught me and made me feel more understanding about the way God feels toward us, the trees of his planting. He prepares the ground and does everything and provides for all that we need to grow and bear fruit to his glory. His heart warms up and is thrilled when we shoot forth our leaves and blossom and bear fruit in righteousness.

And like my mango tree that didn't survive the winter, some of us trees of God will fold at the trials and difficulties that come our way no matter how rich the soil or how much care is provided us by the heavenly gardener.

Let us have our roots go deep into the riches of his grace. Let us avail ourselves of the many things God has provided for our nurture. And let us blossom and bear forth fruit for his glory.

Just Trust His Heart

MANY TIMES, WE don't recognize God's answer to our prayers just because they do not come in the package we have anticipated or in the size and shape we have asked for. This happens because we do not know what is best for us and are unaware of our greatest need. God who knows everything about us and who loves us as a father cherishes his children gives to us not according to our desires but according to what he sees is best for us. Thus, the need to simply trust in God.

God also wants to work with us. He wants us to partner with him even in our work of character development. He sometimes allows us to experience certain things that are difficult and tough when he sees that they would help in refining and perfecting our characters.

In the end, we will see and understand why God did certain things, and we will recognize that God was right after all and that all the time he was making sure that we obtained the greatest and the best. Here is a poem written by an anonymous author that expresses these sentiments.

> I asked for Strength…
> And God gave me Difficulties to make me strong.
> I asked for Wisdom…
> And God gave me Problems to solve.
> I asked for Prosperity…
> And God gave me Brain and Brawn to work.
> I asked for Courage…
> And God gave me Danger to overcome.

I asked for Love...
And God gave me Troubled people to help.
I asked for Favors...
And God gave me Opportunities.
I received nothing I wanted...
I received everything I needed.
Trust in God.

They won't be the things that we desired or wanted in the first place. But we will be satisfied because these are all that we needed, fresh from the hands of God.

Two Wolves

AN OLD CHEROKEE grandfather talked with his grandson who came to him full of anger. A friend had done him an injustice.

"Let me tell you a story," the grandfather said. "I too, at times, have felt a great hatred for those that have done me wrong, with no remorse for what they have done. But hate wears you down. It does not hurt your enemy.

"It is like taking poison and wishing your enemy would die. I have struggled with these feelings many times. It is as if there are two wolves inside me. One is good and does no harm. He lives in harmony with all around him, and does not take offense when no offense was intended. He will only fight when it is right to do so, and in the right way.

"But the other wolf...he is full of anger. The littlest thing will set him into a fit of temper. He fights everyone, all the time, for no reason. He cannot think because his anger and hate are so great. It is helpless anger for his anger will change nothing.

"Sometimes, it is hard to live with these two wolves inside me for both of them try to dominate my spirit."

The boy looked into his grandfather's eyes and asked, "Which one wins, grandfather?"

The grandfather smiled and quietly said, "The one I feed."

This story about the two wolves reminds us of the dilemma the apostle Paul expressed when he said, "For the good that I will to do, I do not do; but the evil I will not to do, that I practice" (Romans 7:19).

And he cries in desperation, "O wretched man that I am! Who will deliver me from this body of death?" (v. 24).

He answers his own desperate question by saying, "I thank God through Jesus Christ our Lord." (v. 25).

So only in Jesus can we find hope of deliverance from this desperation we find ourselves in—caught between our sinful nature and our changed nature that we receive at conversion when we are born again. This constant battle between the two natures we shall continue to wage until the day of Jesus's appearing to fully deliver us from sin and its power.

That is why the apostle says we must die daily and have this sinful nature be crucified on a daily basis (1 Corinthians 15:31).

But as our story suggests, we can have victory in Jesus when we feed "the good wolf" and starve the other. And he admonishes us that we "do not look at the things that are seen but at the things that are not seen. For the things that are seen are temporary, but the things that are not seen are eternal" (2 Corinthians 4:18).

Come, Rest Awhile

IT WAS SPRING break, and my family took time off to be away from pressing duties and enjoy just being together as family.

We spent the week in Flagstaff, Arizona. Elevation is in the five thousand to seven thousand feet above sea level. Temperatures ranged in the thirties to forties. There was snow, and it was fun watching the snowflakes fall as we drove down the road. Sightseeing was most of what we did considering the environmental conditions plus the fact that the area was so rich with many magnificent and breathtaking views.

Sedona, a city thirty miles south of Flagstaff, is known as Red Rock country. The many spectacular canyons and unique rocky mountain formations were awe-inspiring. We also had the chance to look at the Montezuma Castle and Tuzigoot National Monuments, and other ruins of cliff dwellings built by the Sinagua Indians in the eleventh and twelfth centuries.

And of course, we couldn't afford to miss the granddaddy of all canyons and one of the seven wonders of the natural world, the Grand Canyon, eighty miles north.

The six days seemed too short, and we had to pack up and leave again. As I look back, it seems like it was all a dream. And now the world of reality has set in again. But we had our spirits recharged and our physiques rejuvenated.

This was indeed what Jesus was trying to tell his disciples when he said, "Come ye yourselves apart into a desert place and rest a

while. For there were many coming and going and they had no lei-
sure so much as to eat" (Mark 6:31).

Peter Marshall's prayer is also appropriate at this point:

> In the name of Jesus Christ, who was never in a
>   hurry,
>   We pray O God, that Thou wilt slow us down,
>   for we know that we live too fast.
> With all of eternity before us,
>   make us take time to live—
>   time to get acquainted with Thee,
>   time to enjoy Thy blessings,
>   and time to know each other.
> Through Jesus Christ our Lord. Amen.

We Become What We Think

THE WISE MAN says, "As a man thinks in his heart, so is he" (Proverbs 23:7). It is a law of the mind that we become what we think. What we think is what we are. And what we think we become.

For this reason, the apostle Paul counsels us, "Finally, brethren, whatsoever things are true, whatsoever things are noble, whatsoever things are just, whatsoever things are pure, whatsoever things are lovely, whatsoever things are of good report, if there is any virtue and if there is any praise—think on these things" (Philippians 4:8).

So how about choosing one of the following beautiful thoughts, meditating on it, making it a part of your life, and then moving on to the next until they have all become a part of you.

1. Let go of your worries, fears, or any negative thoughts.
2. Consider how very blessed you are.
3. Every moment of your day is fraught with opportunities to bless others.
4. Communicate with love.
5. Resist the urge to murmur and complain.
6. Take time to smell the roses.
7. Thank God for another day of loving.

Remember, we become what we think.

What Do Teachers Make?

DURING THE LONG summer vacation, students and teachers lose themselves in the enjoyment of carefree days and fun-filled nights. Some may begin to miss the neatly structured days of school and work and actually start looking forward to the beginning of the next school year. Still, others may be approaching a crossroad where they may be considering other options on how they will spend the rest of their lives. Are the sacrifices and the work diligently put forth in the last year worth all the effort? Is it time to go look for another vocation in life?

If you are a teacher or a youth leader, let me share with you some material that could inspire and encourage you to keep on going because it is worth all the effort. You are making a difference in people's lives, and that alone is reason enough to continue.

The dinner guests were sitting around the table discussing life. One man, a CEO, decided to explain the problem with education.

He argued, "What's a kid going to learn from someone who decided his best option in life was to become a teacher?"

He reminded the other dinner guests what is sometimes used as an aside about teachers, "Those who can, do. Those who can't, teach."

To stress his point, he said to another guest, "You're a teacher, Susan. Be honest. What do you make?"

Susan, who had a reputation for honesty and frankness, replied, "You want to know what I make?

"I make kids work harder than they ever thought they could.

"I make a C+ feel like the winner of the Congressional Medal of Honor.

"I make kids sit through forty minutes of study in the hall in absolute silence.

"You want to know what I make?

"I make kids wonder.

"I make them question.

"I make them criticize.

"I make them apologize and mean it.

"I make them write.

"I make them read, read, read.

"I make them show all their work in math and perfect their final drafts in English.

"I make them understand that if you have the brains and follow your heart and if someone ever tries to judge you by what you make must pay no attention because they just didn't learn."

Susan paused and then continued, "You want to know what I make?

"I MAKE A DIFFERENCE! Now, what do you make?"

Your Children Might Need to Use It

A FARMER GOT so old that he couldn't work the fields anymore. So he would spend the day just sitting on the porch. His son, still working the farm, would look up from time to time and see his father sitting there.

"He's of no use anymore," the son thought to himself. "He doesn't do anything!"

One day, the son got so frustrated by this that he built a wood coffin, dragged it over the porch, and told his father to get in. Without saying anything, the father climbed inside. After closing the lid, the son dragged the coffin to the edge of the farm where there was a high cliff. As he approached the drop, he heard a light tapping on the lid from inside the coffin. He opened it up. Still lying there peacefully, the father looked up at his son.

"I know you are going to throw me over the cliff, but before you do, may I suggest something?" the father said.

"What is it?" replied the son.

"Throw me over the cliff, if you like," said the father, "but save this good wood coffin. Your children might need to use it."

This is a story that comes with lessons aplenty for all of us. As we live our lives on earth, we get to the point when we are no longer able to do what we want to do or what we even need to do. Some, even among our family, friends, and loved ones, may think we are no longer of any use and are just a burden and a source of irritation and frustration on account of our uselessness. And while some may wish to isolate us, dispose of us, or consign us to oblivion, they forget the fact that actions today will come back sooner or later.

"What goes around comes around" is a truism that has been proven time and time again. It is a law of nature, and in fact, it is a principle that has its roots in scripture. The apostle Paul wrote, "Be not deceived, God is not mocked; for whatsoever a man sows that shall he also reap" (Galatians 6:7).

Let us be loving, kind, and patient to everyone, especially to those who are no longer able to contribute to society and finding it a challenge to even just take care of themselves. Let us sow kind words and deeds and let us prepare ourselves for a bountiful and joyful harvest.

Doing Good and Expecting Nothing in Return

HUMAN NATURE IS selfish. We do good because we want something in return. We entertain people and expect to be entertained by them. We ask them out to lunch, hoping that they return us the favor.

So what happens when the expected response to the good we did does not happen? We get disappointed and vow never to do them a favor again.

We need to realize that a good and kind act is itself its own reward. Because when we do something good and kind, something resonates in us, and we experience a joy that truly satisfies.

Thus, happiness is ours regardless of the response of the intended recipient. And more than this feeling of satisfaction deep within, we know that God himself has his rewards for us in *that* day.

Someone penned the following words:

> It is very important for everyone to have smiled
> at a stranger,
> to have helped somebody they will never see
> again,
> to have done something kind and/or nice for
> somebody with no strings attached, and to
> have loved somebody unconditionally.

There will always come a time, sooner or later,
    when each of us will feel that we have noth-
    ing left to give to this world, or that that this
    world has everything and does not need any-
    thing more from us.

At that time, only if we have done the above,
    will we be able to believe that this world is
    still capable of smiling at us,
    helping us, being kind and nice to us, and
    above all, is capable of loving us.

Truly this world is, to us all, a mirror of our inner selves. Jesus said, "Be not deceived, God is not mocked; whatsoever a man sows that he will also reap" (Galatians 6:7).

We all need the robe of Christ's righteousness, which in the words of Ellen G. White is, "woven in the loom of heaven." It is a garment that is free from the stain of self. We ought to give up our own righteousness and ask for his because as she says, "Even our good works are tainted with our own selfishness."

Let us all give up our own righteousness that the Bible describes are "like filthy rags" and be clothed with the spotless robe of Christ's.

The Greatest Challenge in Life

SOMEONE HAS SAID that the greatest challenge of the human experience is discovering who we really are. And the second greatest is living in a way that honors what we have discovered.

This search for one's identity goes beyond Socrates and continues to the root of all philosophy. "Who am I?" "Where did I come from?" and "Where am I going?" are questions men have asked since the beginning of time.

We are grateful that the Word of God is clear. It tells us exactly who we are, why we are here, and where we are going. And it plainly tells us how we ought to live or what our lives should be like that would honor our God-appointed identity.

Among the descriptions in the scriptures of who we are is that found in the first epistle of Peter 2:9, "But you are a chosen generation, a royal priesthood, a holy nation, a peculiar people, that you should show forth the praises of him who hath called you out of darkness into his marvelous light."

In a nutshell, the preceding passage of scripture tells us who we are and shows how we should live so that we could honor our divine calling and appointment.

The question we need to answer is, "Have we discovered who we are? And are we living in a way that honors this discovery?"

The Thirty-Minute Rule

THERE IS SOMETHING we can do not only to maintain our balance, enjoy life more and for longer years, and be more effective as we minister and serve others. It is called the "Thirty-Minute Rule."

It is described in the following words:

No matter how busy you are, take a half hour each day just for yourself. Go for a walk, plan healthy meals, or simply relax and recharge. You're not being selfish—you need the time to focus on your well-being. After all, if you're not healthy, how can you take care of anyone else?

Come to think about it, this is why the wise and beneficent Creator gave us the night so we can have time for rest and recovery.

And this, too, is why he gave us the Sabbath so that one day in seven we can have the same blessings of rest and spiritual refreshment.

And this also was why Jesus told his disciples, "Come ye yourselves in a desert place and rest awhile... For there were many coming and going and they did not even have time to eat" (Mark 6:31).

Contending for the Faith

IN HIS BOOK *Almost Home*, Elder Ted Wilson, Seventh-day Adventist world church president, calls attention to the fact that we are living in the closing moments of earth's history. As such, he urges members to have a faith on fire for the Lord. He quotes Jude 3 that says that believers should contend for the faith that was once delivered to the saints.

Believers need to have their faith on fire in every area of their lives—be it in their behavior, stewardship, scientific pursuits, dress and deportment, personal relationships, or in their entertainment.

And as far as entertainment goes, there is need for discernment and judiciousness in the choices we make; otherwise, the enemy will take advantage, and we find ourselves corrupted rather than recreated by our pursuits. One of the ways he does this is through TV, and it is not just in the use or misuse of our time but more importantly in the programs that we watch.

Following is an anonymous poem that deals with what happens so many times in the lives of God's professed people.

The Bible and the TV Guide

They lie on the table, side by side,
The Holy Bible and the TV Guide.
One is well worn, but cherished with pride,
Not the Bible, but the TV Guide.
One is used daily to help folks decide,

Not the Bible…it's the TV Guide.
As the pages are turned, what shall they see,
Oh, what does it matter? turn on the TV.
Then confusion reigns, they can't all agree,
On what they shall watch on the old TV.
So they open the book in which they confide,
No, not the Bible…it's the TV Guide
The Word of God is seldom read,
Maybe a verse e'er they fall into bed.
Exhausted and sleepy and tired as can be…
Not from reading the Bible but from watching
TV.
So then back to the table, side by side,
Lay the Holy Bible and the TV Guide.
No time for prayer…no time for the Word,
The plan of salvation is seldom heard.
But forgiveness of sin so full and free,
Is found in the Bible…NOT on TV!

A Layperson's Ten Commandments

WHAT I WANT to share with you is by no means anything that may compare to the Ten Commandments of God's law or something that even comes close to it. They are simply observations that one has made about life, and they are worth considering if we are to find success and a more meaningful experience in our spiritual journey.

They do not need extra explanation as they are self-explanatory, and suffice it to say, they are based on principles from God's Word, and our own spiritual experience are a testimony to their truth and veracity. Here are the following:

1. Prayer is not a "spare wheel" that you pull out when in trouble, but it is a "steering wheel" that directs to the right path throughout the journey.

2. So why is a car's *windshield* so large and the rearview mirror so small? Because our *past* is not as important as our *future*. So look ahead and move on.

3. Friendship is like a *book*. It takes a few minutes to burn, but it takes years to write.

4. All things in life are temporary. If it's going well, enjoy it, they will not last forever. If it's going wrong, don't worry, they can't last long either.

5. Old friends are gold! New friends are diamond! If you get a diamond, don't forget the gold! Because to hold a diamond, you always need a base of gold!

6. Often when we lose hope and think this is the end, GOD smiles from above and says, "Relax, sweetheart, it's just a bend, not the end!"

7. When GOD solves your problems, you have faith in *his* abilities; when GOD doesn't solve your problems, *he* has faith in your abilities.

8. A blind person asked St. Anthony, "Can there be anything worse than losing eyesight?" He replied, "Yes, losing your vision!"

9. When you pray for others, God listens to you and blesses them, and sometimes, when you are safe and happy, remember that someone has prayed for you.

10. *Worrying* does not take away tomorrow's *troubles*. It takes away today's *peace*.

May we lead prayerful lives. And along with a network of supportive friends, let us put all our trust in God, allowing him to take care of our troubles and moving on in faith to a glorious future that he has laid in store for us.

He Paid It All

EVERY TIME WE celebrate communion, we spend time focusing on the passion of Christ. We are reminded of the reason why he came to earth so that he could die and pay the penalty for our sins. And thus he could offer the gift of eternal life to everyone who believes in him as Lord and Savior of their lives.

He also offers us abundant life now. He wants us to live life to its fullest, enjoying the blessings of perfect peace and joy as a result of sins forgiven.

Are we availing ourselves of these blessings? Or maybe, we don't live the abundant life because we don't give it all up to God when we come with our burdens and cares to him.

The following poem brings up this thought.

Broken Dreams

As children bring their broken toys
With tears for us to mend,
I brought my broken dreams to God
Because he was my friend.
But then instead of leaving him
In peace to work alone,
I hung around and tried to help
With ways that were my own.
At last I snatched them back and cried,

"How could you be so slow"
"My child," he said, "What could I do?
You never did let go."

—Author Unknown

Are Your Riches Taxable?

A TAX ASSESSOR came one day to a poor Christian to determine the amount of taxes he would have to pay. The following conversation took place:

"What property do you possess?" asked the assessor.

"I am a very wealthy man," replied the Christian.

"List your possessions please," the assessor instructed.

The Christian said,

"First, I have everlasting life, John 3:16.

"Second, I have a mansion in heaven, John 14:2.

"Third, I have peace that passes all understanding, Philippians 4:7.

"Fourth, I have joy unspeakable, 1 Peter 1:8.

"Fifth, I have divine love that never fails, 1 Corinthians 13:8.

"Sixth, I have a faithful wife, Proverbs 31:10.

"Seventh, I have healthy, happy, obedient children, Exodus 20:12.

"Eighth, I have true, loyal friends, Proverbs 18:24.

"Ninth, I have songs in the night, Psalm 42:8.

"Tenth, I have a crown of life, James 1:12."

The tax assessor closed his book and said, "Truly, you are a very rich man, but your property is not subject to taxation."

Let us all strive to possess this kind of riches that is not subject to taxes because these are heavenly treasures, and they are all that matter now and for all eternity.

At the Lord's Clinic

THE FOLLOWING PARABLE bares our spiritual condition and suggests what we might do to live a healthy, spiritual lifestyle.

Here it goes:

> I went to the Lord's Clinic to have my routine checkup, and I confirmed I was ill.
>
> When Jesus took my blood pressure, He saw I was low in tenderness.
>
> When He read my temperature, the thermometer registered 40 degrees of anxiety.
>
> He ran an electrocardiogram and found that I needed several "love bypasses" since my arteries were blocked with loneliness and could not provide for an empty heart.
>
> I went to orthopedics, because I could not walk by my brother's side and I could not hug my friends, since I had fractured myself when tripping with envy.
>
> He also found that I was short-sighted, since I could not see beyond the shortcomings of my brothers and sisters.
>
> When I complained about deafness, the diagnosis was that I had stopped listening to Jesus' voice talking to me on a daily basis.

For all of that, Jesus gave me a free consultation
thanks to His mercy, so my pledge is,
Once I leave this clinic, only to take the natural
remedies He prescribed through His words
of truth:
Every morning, take a full glass of gratitude.
When getting to work, take one spoon of peace.
Every hour, take one pill of patience, one cup of
brotherhood and one glass of humility.
When getting home, take one dose of love.
When getting to bed, take two caplets of clear
conscience.

May we all be blessed as we allow the Great Physician to search
us, try us, and restore us to the abundant life he wants all of us to
have.

Are You Happy?

CHRISTIANS ARE SUPPOSED to be the happiest people in the world. And this is because of our assurance of eternal life and the message of healthful living that we have had all along.

Of course, it is one thing to believe; quite another thing to put these principles into practice. So if you think you are missing out on life, and you want to know how you can live life to the full, why not try the following simple suggestions on how to be happy.

Twelve Ways to Be Happy

1. Make up your mind to be happy. Learn to find pleasure in simple things.
2. Make the best of your circumstances. No one has everything, and everyone has something of sorrow intermingled with gladness of life. The trick is to make the laughter outweigh the tears.
3. Don't take yourself too seriously. Don't think that somehow you should be protected from misfortune that befalls other people.
4. You can't please everybody. Don't let criticism worry you.
5. Don't let your neighbor set your standards. Be yourself.
6. Do the things you enjoy doing but stay out of debt.
7. Never borrow trouble. Imaginary things are harder to bear than real ones.

8. Since hate poisons the soul, do not cherish jealousy. Avoid people who make you unhappy.
9. Have many interests. If you can't travel, read about new places.
10. Don't hold postmortems. Don't spend your time brooding over sorrows and mistakes. Don't be one who never gets over things.
11. Do what you can for those less fortunate than yourself.
12. Keep busy at something. A busy person never has time to be unhappy.

And I could add one more, albeit the most important one, in the mix of happiness in life.

13. To know lasting happiness, get to know Jesus. In the final analysis, knowing Jesus in a personal way as Savior and Lord is the secret of true and lasting happiness. Like the bumper sticker that says, "Know Jesus, know peace (and happiness). No Jesus, no peace (and happiness)."

Do You Know What is Truth?

MAY 21, 2011, was a great disappointment for a group of believers who were waiting to be "raptured" to glory on that day. Reporters say that Harold Camping who made the prediction was flabbergasted and had no explanation for the failed prophecy. Some followers tried to console themselves by saying God must have delayed the judgment to give time for sinners to repent and so that more could be saved.

It is to be observed that the group's followers were sincere in their faith and belief and wanted to let the world know about it. They spent huge sums of money in billboards across the country and through other media. One group member spent $140,000 of his life savings for this purpose.

But sincerity alone is not enough. When it comes to salvation, you have to know the truth. In this case, the truth is the Bible doesn't teach any "rapture," and as far as the second coming or the end of the world is concerned, no one knows the day and the hour (Matthew 24:42–44).

Without a knowledge of what is the truth, one is likely to be deceived. It is time we got serious with Bible truth for the spirit of prophecy says, none but those who fortify their minds with the truths of scripture will be able to stand in the last great conflict/in the last days.

Reaching Out and Sharing

AT OUR WEDNESDAY night evenings, we have recently begun a series of studies on the virtue of hospitality. This is a very important Christian virtue if rightly understood and practiced. It can revitalize our individual lives and bring new life and energy to any congregation.

This is why apostle Peter instructs us to use hospitality one to another without grudging (1 Peter 4:8–9), and the apostle Paul tells Titus and Timothy that those who desire to be elders must be given to hospitality or be a lover of hospitality (1 Timothy 3:1–2, Titus 1:7–9).

The Greek word used for hospitality is *philoxenos* that literally means "to reach out to strangers." And because in a sense, we are all strangers to each other. We need to open our hearts, our hands, and our homes, and share our lives with each other. So hospitality is "reaching out and touching someone" as AT&T would like us to do.

There is a poem entitled "When We Share" written by an anonymous author, and it shows us what actually happens when we reach out and share our lives with one another.

When we share laughter,	If we share a smile
There's twice the fun;	Then our love shows;
When we share success	If we share a hug,
We surpass what we have done.	Then our love grows.

When we share problems,
There's half the pain;
When we share tears,
A rainbow follows rain.

When we share dreams,
They become more real;
When we share secrets,
It's our hearts we reveal.

If we share with someone,
On whom we depend;
That person becomes
Family or friend.

And what draws us closer,
And makes us all care;
Is not what we have
But the things we share.

Celebrating Mother's Day

MOTHER'S DAY IS a time for commemoration and celebration for moms. It is a time for breakfasts in bed, family get-togethers, and crayon-scribbled "I Love Yous." Here is a poem that I like to share with mothers, and I hope it will give them joy not only today but the whole year through.

If I could give you diamonds
　　for each tear you cried for me,
If I could find you sapphires
　　for each truth you've helped me see,
If I could give you rubies
　　for the heartache that you've known,
If I could give you pearls
　　for the wisdom that you've shown-

Then you'll have a treasure, mother,
　　that would mount up to the skies
that would almost match the sparkle
　　in your kind and loving eyes.

But I have no pearls, sapphires, rubies or diamonds,
　　As I'm sure you're well aware
So I'll give you gifts more precious-
　　My DEVOTION, LOVE AND CARE.

I hope that the sentiment of this poem is shared by every child because, hey, moms do deserve everything that we can give them in appreciation for all they do and all they mean to all of us.

Mothers' Value through the Years

MOTHERS ARE NOT always valued for who they really are. They are recognized, but their value seems to fluctuate in the perception of a child through the development years. In the end, we realize how much they are really worth, but sad to say, it usually comes when it is too late, and they may already be gone.

As a matter of fact, they deserve all the accolades their families can heap on them for their love, kindness, and sacrificial spirit.

The following material illustrates how mothers are perceived through the years in a child's life.

Images of Mother

Four years of age—my mom can do anything!
Eight years of age—my mom knows a lot! A whole lot!
Twelve years of age—my mom doesn't understand me.
Fifteen years of age—my mom doesn't let me do anything.
Eighteen years of age—I'm an adult. My mom can't control me anymore.
Twenty-five years of age—I should have listened to Mom.
Thirty-five years of age—before we decide, let's get Mom's opinion.
Fifty years of age—I wonder what Mom would have thought about it.
Sixty-five years of age—I wish I could talk it over with Mom.

Mothers are the best thing that ever happened to families. Let's give them our love and appreciation. They deserve the best.

The Real Tribute to Mothers

WHEN MOTHER'S DAY comes around, Moms are given preferential treatment as children express their love in celebration of the special day. There will be cards and affirmations of affection in appreciation for what mothers do to make the home and family life a place where we all want to be.

But the real tribute to mothers is not what we say on Mother's Day but what we do every day of the year.

The poem that follows brings out this thought.

I love you, Mother, said little Nell
I love you more than tongues can tell.
Then teased and pouted for half the day
Till her mother rejoiced when she went to play.

I love you, Mother, said little John
Forgetting his work, his cap went on.
Then he was off to the garden swing
Leaving his mother the wood to bring.

I love you, Mother, said little Ann
Today I'll help you all I can
Then stepping softly, she took the broom
Swept the floor and tidied the room.

I love you, Mother, again they said
Three little children all going to bed.
Now which one do you suppose really loved
Mother the most?

It's like Jesus's parable of the two sons in Matthew 21:28–31. A man came to the first and said, "Son, go, work today in my vineyard." He answered and said, "I will not," but afterward, he regretted it and went. Then he came to the second and said likewise. And he answered and said, "I go," but he did not go.

And Jesus asks, "Which of the two did the will of his father?"

In the final analysis, it's not what we say but what we do that determines the quality of our love and devotion whether it is for our mothers on earth or for our Father in heaven.

Let us say it and do it with love.

The Power of a Mother's Love

ABOUT 6:00 A.M. on a Wednesday morning, James Lawson of Running Springs, California, (in the San Bernardino mountains) left home to apply for a job. About an hour later, his thirty-six-year-old wife, Patsy, left for her fifth-grade teaching job down the mountain in Riverside—accompanied by her two children, five-year-old Susan and two-year-old Gerald—to be dropped off at the babysitter's. Unfortunately, they never got that far. Eight and a half hours later, the man found his wife and daughter dead in their wrecked car, upside down in a cold mountain stream. His two-year-old son was just barely alive in the forty-eight-degree water.

But in that death, the character of a mother was revealed in a most dramatic and heart-rending way. For when the father scrambled down the cliff to what he was sure were the cries of his dying wife, he found her locked in death, holding her little boy's head just above water in the submerged car. For eight and a half hours, Patsy Lawson had held her beloved toddler afloat and had finally died. Her body was almost frozen in death in the position of self-giving love, holding her baby up to breathe. She died that another might live. That's the essence of a mother's love.

Certainly, among all the human emotions, a mother's love is arguably the one that approximates God's love the most. For that reason, an ancient Jewish proverb says, "God could not be everywhere and therefore He made mothers."

We pay tribute to all the mothers. Thank you for all you do to make our homes a little heaven on earth and our lives a whole lot sweeter.

Conversation with God

WHEN FAMILY MEMBERS and loved ones pass away, sorrow and grief come like a cloud over us, and no doubt generate in-depth conversations between us and God. And during times like these, the question invariably comes up, "Why?"

Of course, generally, we know the reason for suffering and death. It is because of sin that we suffer and die. These are all part of life on this sin-infested planet. But from the beginning, it wasn't so. God had planned to have a world of perfect peace and happiness that would go on forever.

But as to the specifics to the answer of why suffering and death, we do not know. We will know at a later time, and God himself will make it plain to us. For now, it will be sufficient to know that God sees our pain. He understands our grief and loss. And he gives us the strength and the courage to live in these trying and difficult moments of our lives.

An unnamed author talks about how a loving God understands and comforts us in our grief.

I said, "God, I hurt."
And God said, "I know."
I said, "God, I cry a lot."
And God said, "That's why I gave you tears."
I said, "God, I am so depressed."
And God said, "That is why I gave you sunshine."
I said, "God, life is so hard."
And God said, "That is why I gave you loved ones."

I said, "God, my loved one died."
And God said, "So did mine."
I said, "God, it is such a loss."
And God said, "I saw mine nailed to a cross."
I said, "God, your loved one lives."
And God said, "So will yours."
I said, "God, it hurts."
And God said, "I know."

The Cracked Pot

AN ELDERLY CHINESE woman had two large pots; each hung on the ends of a pole that she carried across her neck. One of the pots had a crack in it while the other pot was perfect and always delivered a full portion of water. At the end of the long walk from the stream to the house, the cracked pot arrived only half full.

For a full two years, this went on daily with the woman bringing home only one and a half pots of water. Of course, the perfect pot was proud of its accomplishments. But the poor cracked pot was ashamed of its own imperfection and miserable that it could only do half of what it had been made to do.

After two years of what it perceived to be bitter failure, it spoke to the woman one day by the stream. "I am ashamed of myself because this crack in my side causes water to leak out all the way back to your house."

The old woman smiled and said, "Did you notice that there are flowers on your side of the path but not on the other pot's side? That's because I have always known about your flaw, so I planted flower seeds on your side of the path, and every day while we walk back, you water them."

"For two years, I have been able to pick these beautiful flowers to decorate the table. Without you being just the way you are, there would not be this beauty to grace us."

Each of us has our own unique flaw. But it's the cracks and flaws we each have that make our lives together so very interesting and rewarding. You've just got to take each person for what they are and look for the good in them. So to all of my cracked pot friends, have a great day and remember to smell the flowers on your side of the path!

Do You Want to Be Happy?

SOMETIMES IN LIFE'S journey, we come to a dead end. Life loses its meaning, and we get discouraged. We think that life is no longer worth living. Things that used to excite us have become a bore. Even the best that life can offer don't matter anymore.

Here's a poem that suggests what we can do to get back that zest for living we once had.

How to Be Happy

Are you almost disgusted with life, little man?
    I'll tell you a wonderful trick
That will bring you contentment, if anything can,
    Do something for somebody, quick!

Are you awfully tired with play, little girl?
    Wearied, discouraged, and sick—
I'll tell you the loveliest game in the world,
    Do something for somebody, quick!

Though it rains, like the rain of the flood, little man,
    And the clouds are forbidding and thick,
You can make the sun shine in your soul, little man,
    Do something for somebody, quick!

Though the stars are like brass overhead, little girl,
  And the walks like a well-heated brick,
And our earthly affairs in a terrible whirl,
  Do something for somebody, quick!

And you wonder why this is true? Jesus says, "If you have done it to the least of these my brethren, you have done it unto Me" (Matthew 25:40).

In the final analysis, loving and serving the Lord (that means doing something for someone) is what brings happiness in life because that is why we have been created and why we are here in this world.

And happiness comes when we fulfill the purpose of our creation.

Our Responsibility Is in the Telling

STEVE BROWN WRITES this way as he deals with the subject of taking responsibility for what we need to take responsibility on:

I feel that God has put me beside a cliff where people dance close to the edge. I say to them, "Look, if I were you I wouldn't get so close. I have seen people go over, and they always get hurt. Some of them get killed."

And they say, "I really appreciate your telling me that. I didn't realize it was so dangerous."

And then they jump!

I feel so responsible for the pain. And the Father reminds me through his Word, "Son, you are not responsible for the jumping. You are responsible for the telling. As long as you are faithful, you don't have to play God."

God has commanded us to go and give the message. He has commissioned us to be watchmen on the walls of Zion to warn people of their sins. He has instructed us to show them the way to salvation and eternal life. Obviously, some will receive the message gladly while others will oppose or simply be apathetic. And we sometimes feel responsibility for the choices they make.

This is where we need to realize that we can't take responsibility for decisions people make. Our responsibility is the telling, the warning, the sharing. When we come to their homes with the message, and they shut their doors on us, and when we try to reach out to them, and their minds remain closed, we have done our part.

And let us just be faithful to that which God has asked us to do.

China: Land of Culture, Enchantment, and Spectacular Beauty

I HAD THE special privilege of spending my vacation on a tour of China. And the two weeks I spent there with many friends erased any negative image I had of this country. Growing up, I had thoughts of China as someplace where the communists live, and you know, the communists are "bad" people. This trip went far beyond my expectations as I found the place very beautiful and enchanting, and the people very law-abiding, very disciplined, honest, clean, and very nice.

One impressive thing is the culture and civilization that have been their heritage dating back to hundreds of years before Christ. The Great Wall is one of the most amazing feats of mankind, spanning over four thousand miles over high mountains and intricate passes. Its length, height, and width boggle the imagination as one thinks of how these people tried to protect themselves from enemy invaders coming from north of their border.

The thousands of life-sized Terracotta Warriors dug from around an early emperor's grave at Xi'an is one of the most amazing discoveries of modern times and may have a rightful claim to the title "Eighth Wonder of the World." It speaks not only of man's desire to continue life after death but also details Chinese military strategy and prowess in ancient times.

The mighty Yangtze River, third longest river in the world, is another natural wonder as it winds its way from Tibet in the north, cutting across central China, and spilling its waters into the China Sea near Shanghai in the south. Cruising along the dark green waters of the river was one memorable experience as we sailed through narrow gorges of mountains towering in the sky, observing monkeys, and other wildlife in their natural habitat, seeing hanging coffins up on the cliffs, and enjoying the yellow blooming canolas in terraced fields that stretched like giant stairways in the sky.

Throughout the trip, we spoke of how we were so impressed by this great country and its people. But during our final worship service at our hotel conference room in Shanghai (our first worship service was on top of the Great Wall in Beijing), our thoughts were centered on how we could share our message to the 1.3 billion people in this land, one-fourth of the world's population, who do not know Christ. We felt that the Lord was speaking to all of us about this challenge, and we talked lengthily about it.

Meanwhile, I think I'll just continue to faithfully do the task of telling my neighbors here in Los Angeles about my crucified, risen, and soon coming Savior.

Thoughts for Daily Living

I WANT TO share with you some inspiring and thought-provoking statements that I have come across in my reading. They are full of meaning and cover various subjects such as the prayer life, emotional and spiritual maturity, and a variety of things that we deal with from day to day.

How do you like the following?

1. God wants spiritual fruit, not religious nuts.
2. Dear God, I have a problem: It's *me.*
3. Growing old is inevitable... Growing *up* is optional
4. There is no key to happiness. The door is always open.
5. Silence is often misinterpreted but never misquoted.
6. Do the math... Count your blessings.
7. Faith is the ability to *not* panic.
8. Laugh every day. It's like internal jogging.
9. If you worry, you didn't pray. If you pray, don't worry.
10. As a child of God, prayer is kind of like calling home every day.
11. Blessed are the flexible for they shall not be bent out of shape.
12. The most important things in your home are the people.
13. When we get tangled up in our problems, be still. God wants us to be still so *he* can untangle the knot.
14. A grudge is a heavy thing to carry.
15. He who dies with the most toys is still dead.

Watch the Children

Do you sometimes feel that you have gotten stuck in a rut, and everything is a meaningless routine? You get bored going through the motions. It's like you have come to a dead end in your career, and you have nothing to look forward to. You have lost all zest for living.

Joseph J. Mazzella gives a suggestion in the following material. He says that watching little children play and enjoy their simple, uncluttered lives gives us a perspective on life that is seen through the eyes of hope, wonder, and simplicity.

"Each day just before I pick up my boy, I take in this glorious and happy sight of the preschool children having one last recess before they go home. Many of the parents are there as well smiling as they watch that special joy that their children are creating. I look on as one happy boy swings and calls out for his teacher to watch. I see two smiling girls skip, laugh, and gather handfuls of dandelions to give their moms. I watch as two boys ride the rocking horses with all the energy and delight that their little hearts can muster. I smile upon seeing a girl hanging upside down from the miniature monkey bars and giggling at the whole world. As I get my own son, he too runs for the swing set for one last ride as well before we head home. He may have the body of a twelve-year-old, but he still has the bliss of a child's heart, mind, and soul.

These beautiful children remind me every day that life truly is about joy, laughter, and love. Anything else is just details. We may all have to go to our jobs, clean our homes, raise our families, and take care of all the tasks in life. Still, there is no reason we can't do all these things with love, laughter, and joy.

In fact, the only thing we should take seriously in this life is the love and joy that we choose and share. It is what makes life worth living, and it is God's greatest gift to us all. Cherish that gift then. Rejoice in it. Share it with the world. And if you don't think you can remember how to, then stop by a playground one day and watch the children."

Jesus himself says, "Unless you are converted and become as little children, you will by no means enter the kingdom of heaven" (Matthew 18:3). The simplicity, humility, and confiding trust of a little child are characteristic traits we need to have, without which, we can't enter the kingdom of heaven.

But we can learn even more from little kids. Their sense of wonder and appreciation of what life offers them each day are things we can learn as we rediscover that life is still worth living for us and those we care about.

Offending the Little Children

AN OLD WOMAN was noticed to be picking up something in the street—a poor slum street. The policeman on the beat noticed the woman's action and watched her suspiciously. Several times, he saw her stoop, pick up something, and hide it in her apron. Finally, he went up to her, and with a gruff voice and threatening manner demanded, "What are you carrying off in your apron?"

The timid woman did not answer at first, whereupon the officer, thinking that she must have found something valuable, threatened her with arrest. The woman opened her apron and revealed a handful of broken glasses. "I just thought I would like to take it out of the way of the children's feet," she said.

Should we have more among us of this timid little woman who cared about what hurts "children's feet?"

One of the most arresting statements of Jesus when he was on earth was concerning the offending of little children. He said, "Whoever causes any of these little ones who believe in Me to sin, it would be better for him if a millstone were hung around his neck and he were drowned in the depths of the sea" (Matthew 18:6).

Let us make sure not to offend any of these little ones and not cause them to stumble by our example or our words.

Youth and the Church

LET US BE encouraging and supportive of our youth. They are not just the future of the church. They are the life of the church *now*. We want them to know that they have ownership of the church and its programs *now* together with all the rest of the more mature members of the congregation.

In the inaugural message of General Conference president Robert Folkenberg at the world session of Seventh-day Adventists at Indianapolis in 1990, he expressed concern for the youth of the church. He talked about how many of them were leaving the church and getting lost to the world. He visualized the church as one great big family and suggested that perhaps, if we gave our youth a "piece of the pie, they are going to stay for dinner."

So we need to do this, and we need to do what we can *now*. Tomorrow may be too late. Below is a short but meaningful poem that talks about the opportunities we have with your youth *now*.

> They pass so quickly, the days of youth,
>   And the children change so fast,
> And soon they harden in the mold,
>   And the plastic years are past.
>
> Then shape their lives while they are young,
>   This be our prayer, our aim,
> That every child we meet shall bear
>   The imprint of His name.

A Prayer for Our Children

OUR CHILDREN ARE a heritage from the Lord. And it is his desire that we not only take good care of them but to train them to love and serve him. We realize that this is not an easy task because the enemy of our souls is out to get them and wants to send them to their ruin.

They are exposed to so many temptations. The world around them threatens to engulf and cast them into its own mold. But let us not be discouraged because God himself is on our side. And as the scripture says, "He who is in you is greater than he who is in the world" (1 John 4:4).

As we realize the seriousness of the battle for our children, let us turn to God and let him preserve and protect our little ones. And even for those among our youth that may have been led astray by the evil one, let us continue to pray for them. Let us have faith that God hears our prayers. He will bring them back and will help us overcome because he is greater than any of our foes and bigger than any of our problems.

A poem written by Amy Carmichael encourages us to do this. Let the following prayer be in the heart and lips of parents and let God show himself powerful again as he proves himself faithful to his Word.

Father, hear us, we are praying.
Hear the words our hearts are saying.
We are praying for our children.

Keep them from the powers of evil,
From the secret, hidden peril.
Father, hear us for our children.

From the worldling's hollow gladness,
From the sting of faithless sadness,
Father, Father, keep our children.

Through life's troubled waters steer them.
Through life's bitter battles cheer them.
Father, Father, be thou near them.

And wherever they may bide,
Lead them home at eventide.

The Things That Really Matter

EVERY NOW AND then, we celebrate our achievements in school, at work, or in life in general. We throw parties, organize a parade, or plan a special program to commemorate and savor the sweetness of success. We also want to reward the hard work, determination, and persistence of those that triumphed and recognize the parents and other family members and friends who have been a network of support to them in their undertakings.

To those who have attained success and to everyone journeying on the road of life, I want to share this thought with you. Ralph Waldo Emerson once said,

> What lies behind us and what lies before us
>   are tiny matters
> Compared to what lies within us.

Whether you continue to prepare and train yourself for life's greater challenges or are trying to find your place in the sun, what you have achieved and what may be ahead of you are not going to be of utmost importance. What matters most is what you have inside of you—your character. And the quality of character you have developed to this moment in time will spell success or failure in this life and in the life to come.

The prophet Jeremiah says it this way:

Thus says the Lord:
"Let not the wise man glory in his wisdom,
Let not the mighty man glory in his might,
Nor let the rich man glory in his riches;
But let him who glories glory in this,
That he understands and knows Me,
That I am the Lord, exercising loving kindness,
judgment and righteousness in the earth.
For in these I delight," says the Lord.

—Jeremiah 9:23–24

May God continue to crown your best efforts with success all your lives.

The Purpose of True Education

MARCHING GOWNS AND togas, diplomas, medals, and scholarship awards are all trappings of success in the academic field and the results of hard work and steely determination through the years. Following graduation from school, most will be looking for jobs that will match the skills and training they have acquired through the years.

What all must remember is to be certain they have obtained true education and are fulfilling its very purpose. Education is not a school that we graduate from. In fact, it is something that we get enrolled in for as long as we live while we are on this side of eternity.

In defining what true education is, Ellen G. White says that it is what trains youth and students for the life that now is and the life that is to come (*Fundamentals of True Education*, 327). She also has said that the object of education is "to restore in man the image of his Maker," and "to bring him back to the perfection in which he was created" (*Education*, 15–16).

If education has trained one for life here on earth and prepared him for the life in the earth made new and if in his soul the image of God is being restored and is steadily and surely moving to the perfection in which man was created, then he is experiencing real educational success. And this success is greater than any of the degrees, diplomas, and accolades anyone has earned or will ever achieve in life.

So here is to more success in life's educational pursuits!

What Diplomas Are For

THE CONGRATULATORY GREETINGS and accolades that people receive when they finish school are certainly well deserved. They are a token payoff of the earnest and untiring efforts put forth through the years under the blessing and grace of God.

Parents, family, and friends deserve commendation as well since they provide a reliable support system in the face of all the challenges and obstacles encountered on the road to success.

But when all the parties and celebrations are over, what next?

A segment from a speech of Tom Brokaw as he addressed a group of graduates presents this challenge. It says,

> You are educated. Your certificate is in your degree. You may think of it as a ticket to the good life. Let me ask you to think of an alternative. Think of it as your ticket to change the world.

A diploma, after all, is not just a document that certifies that you have successfully completed the requirements of a certain course or discipline. It is not simply a nice piece of quality paper to hang on and decorate our walls with. It should be taken as something that affirms and validates us in our role as change agents to make this world a better place.

May this world be a better place, our churches more blessed, and our homes a happier place because of our achievement in school. And we have our diplomas on the wall to prove it.

Goals Do Not End with Commencement Exercises

GOALS HAVE A way of spurring one to keep trekking to a destination that may seem to be so far off in the distance. They have a way of making the longed-for object loom larger, sweeter and more desirable. And even when conditions get tough, envisioning the success at the end of the road is what makes the feet go lighter and allows the body to keep pushing one step at a time until one views the finish line.

Goals are what make students in school finish their chosen course of study in due time, if not in record time.

The tragedy is that some who finish their schooling with the help of carefully set goals quit after experiencing the sweet taste of success. They have achieved their goal and that's it. They allow their goals to get buried in the graveyard of graduation exercises, parties, and celebrations.

That should not be the case. There's a lot more to be achieved in life if one has to live it to the fullest. And setting meaningful and reachable goals is part of the excitement of daily living.

So move on and focus on the attainment of life's goals. Keep reaching out for bigger and higher goals. Someone said, "Shoot for the moon. And even if you miss, you'll land among the stars."

Wherever you go, however, take Christ along with you. And no matter how lofty your ambitions are and however high your goals, I trust that they will all be for the glory of God and the blessing of your fellow men.

How Success Is Measured

By DEFINITION, SUCCESS is the achievement of goals that have been set within a certain period of time. These could be in the field of education as when one finishes a certain degree or course of study. It could be in the area of life in general as when one attains financial independence and has enough money to buy a house, a car, and the other necessities of day-to-day living.

As one basks in the glory of the moment of success, it is important to realize what true success really means. How successful can a person be? How is success measured?

Ralph Waldo Emerson says much about this. He talks about the true measure of success in this way:

> How do you measure success?
> To laugh often and much;
> To win the respect of intelligent people
>   and the affection of children;
> To earn the appreciation of honest critics
>   and endure the betrayal of false friends;
> To appreciate beauty;
> To find the best in others;
> To leave the world a bit better
>   whether by a healthy child,
>   a redeemed social condition,
>   or a job well done;

To know even one other life has breathed
because you lived—
this is to have succeeded.

Let me add to the wisdom of Emerson's words that to ultimately succeed in life, one has to know God and his Son Jesus Christ.

In his prayer, Jesus said, "And this is life eternal, that they may know You, the only true God, and Jesus Christ whom You have sent" (John 17:3).

Ultimate success in life therefore is knowing God and his Son Jesus Christ as personal Lord and Savior because this kind of knowledge brings one the gift of eternal life.

Leaving Your Comfort Zone

MARK TWAIN SAID, "Twenty years from now you will be more disappointed by the things that you didn't do than by the ones that you did do. So throw off the bowlines. Sail away from the safe harbor. Catch the trade winds in your sails. Explore. Dream. Discover."

Having achieved a degree of success in life, it is time to go out and make a difference. And as you go, don't be paralyzed by the safety of the familiar. Sail on to heights unknown. Go out and change your world, making it a better place. Do something different. Leave your comfort zone. Do not try to find a path and follow where it leads. Go to where there is no pathway and leave a trail. You can't walk on water if you do not leave the safety of the boat.

Most important of all, of course, is to have God always with you. Go to where he leads because where he wants you to go and what he wants you to be is where success and true and lasting happiness may be found.

When Is a Man Educated?

Joseph Fort Newton asks a question about education and offers a response himself thus, "When is a man educated? When he knows how to live, how to love, how to hope, how to pray, and is not afraid to die."

What he says is interesting and thought-provoking, but I like what Ellen White says about the purpose of true education better when she states, "To restore in man the image of his Maker, to bring him back into the perfection in which he was created—this is the purpose of true education, the real object of life."

So how educated are you? You realize that it is not measured so much by the kind of diploma you have received. It will rather be measured by how fully you reflect the image of God and how close you are to the original perfection wherein man on earth was created.

May you keep moving to that goal through the grace of the Holy Spirit.

Lessons from the School of Life

As WE LIVE each day, we experience life, and we come away with lessons that will not only help us live our lives better and wiser and thus more enjoyable but also prepare us for the higher life that is to come.

St. Paul says we should live our lives in wisdom (Ephesian 5:15) that means we should plan our daily lives and learn from our experiences so we can live wisely.

The following material is attributed to Andy Rooney, a man gifted with saying so much in so few words. He says,

> I've learned… That the best classroom in the world is at the feet of an elderly person.
>
> I've learned… That when you're in love, it shows.
>
> I've learned… That just one person saying to me, "You've made my day!" makes my day.
>
> I've learned… That having a child fall asleep in your arms is one of the most peaceful feelings in the world.
>
> I've learned… That being kind is more important than being right.
>
> I've learned… That you should never say "No" to a gift from a child.
>
> I've learned… That I can always pray for someone when I don't have the strength to help him in any other way.

I've learned… That no matter how serious your life requires you to be, everyone needs a friend to act goofy with.

I've learned… That sometimes all a person needs is a hand to hold and a heart to understand.

I've learned… That simple walks with my father around the block on summer nights when I was a child did wonders for me as an adult.

I've learned… That we should be glad God doesn't give us everything we ask for.

I've learned… That money doesn't buy class.

I've learned… That it's those small daily happenings that make life so spectacular.

I've learned… That under everyone's hard shell is someone who wants to be appreciated and loved.

I've learned… That to ignore the facts does not change the facts.

I've learned… That when you plan to get even with someone, you are only letting that person continue to hurt you.

I've learned… That love, not time, heals all wounds.

I've learned… That the easiest way for me to grow as a person is to surround myself with people smarter than I am.

I've learned… That everyone you meet deserves to be greeted with a smile.

I've learned… That life is tough, but I'm tougher.

I've learned… That opportunities are never lost; someone will take the ones you miss.

I've learned… That when you harbor bitterness, happiness will dock elsewhere.

I've learned… That I wish I could have told my Mom that I love her one more time before she passed away.

I've learned… That one should keep his words both soft and tender, because tomorrow he may have to eat them.

I've learned… That a smile is an inexpensive way to improve your looks.

I've learned… That when your newly born grand-child holds your little finger in his little fist, you're hooked for life.

I've learned… That everyone wants to live on top of the mountain, but all the happiness and growth occurs while you're climbing it.

I've learned… That the less time I have to work with, the more things I get done.

I trust that we've all learned these lessons from the school of life and pick up more as we move on. For to live wisely is to live within the will of God (Ephesians 5:15–17).

Do the Right Thing Anyway

IN THIS WORLD of ours, we find it hard to be good or do good. There are 1,001 reasons why we should follow the crowd and do what is popular—what is politically correct. It is difficult because we find ourselves so alone, and the path we have taken may be so unbeaten, so far removed from the well-travelled paths of ease and convenience. But once we are persuaded that what we believe is right and what we intend to do is in perfect harmony with the revealed will of God, then let us go ahead and do it. For in the end, it wouldn't count how many stood with us. In the final analysis, what is important is whether God was with us for God is always right.

The following material expresses this thought and is taken from Dr. Kent M. Keith's *The Paradoxical Commandments*. Some people have attributed it to Mother Teresa because she had it on the wall of her children's home in Calcutta, India.

Anyway

People are unreasonable, illogical and self-centered.
Love them anyway.
If you do good, people will accuse you of selfish ulterior motives.
Do good anyway.
If you are successful, you win false friends and true enemies.

Succeed anyway.

The good you do today will be forgotten
tomorrow.

Do good anyway.

Honesty and frankness make you vulnerable.

Be honest and frank anyway.

What you spend years building may be destroyed
overnight.

Build anyway.

People really need help but may attack you if you
help them.

Help people anyway.

Give the world the best you have and you'll get
kicked in the teeth.

Give the world the best you've got anyway.

You see, in the final analysis, It is between you
and God;

It was never between you and them anyway.

So in spite of the way things may be going, do the right thing
anyway. And God who sees all and is the ultimate judge of all men's
deeds will see that you get your just reward.

What Is a Dad?

When Father's Day comes around, we express gratitude to God and give appreciation to fathers for faithfully fulfilling their roles and helping make our households places that God delights in.

Dads are a blessing and the following material expands on it.

> A Dad is a mender of toys, a leader of boys.
> He's a changer of fuses, a healer of bruises.
> He's a mover of couches, a healer of ouches.
> He's a hanger of screens, a counselor of teens.
> He's a pounder of nails, a teller of tales.
> He's a dryer of dishes, a fulfiller of wishes.
> Bless him, O Lord.

But more than being a handyman around the house and among the kids, a father's real worth is determined by how much he is able to reflect and model his heavenly Father to his children. For after all, his God-ordained task is to reflect the image of his Father in heaven and make it easier for his children to know their father's heavenly Father.

Congratulations to all the fathers out there for such a challenging and sublime task. And may God grant you his grace to succeed in your ministry to your particular households.

What Makes a Dad

FATHERS ARE TO be recognized for the love, sacrifices, and support that they give to the family. Without them giving of their best, families would not be as happy and blessed.

May God continue to give them health and strength and long life and that they may use their God-given talents and gifts to continue to hold the family close to him.

The poem below that was written by an anonymous author describes how God made the father in the family so that he can be the leader in the home and the provider, protector, and priest for the entire household.

May it give joy and satisfaction and lead to a greater determination to be strong in the task that the heavenly Father has given them.

To all the fathers out there, this poem is dedicated.

> God took the strength of a mountain,
> The majesty of a tree,
> The warmth of a summer sun,
> The calm of a quiet sea,
> The generous soul of nature,
> The comforting arm of night,
> The wisdom of the ages,
> The power of an eagle's flight,
> The joy of morning in spring,
> The faith of a mustard seed,
> The patience of eternity,

The depth of a family need.
Then God combined these qualities,
When there was nothing more to add,
He knew His masterpiece was complete,
And so, He called it… "DAD."

Leading by Example

FATHERS ARE THE heads of the household. They are the leaders in the home and more than anything, they are to bring the children and family up in the nurture and admonition of the Word of God. By both precept and example, they are to teach the children the love of God (Deuteronomy 6:5–7).

The poet Emerson said, "What you are thunders so loud I couldn't hear what you say." That is why fathers (and mothers too) need to model what they teach or children who are trying to walk in their footsteps would get confused. And we need to be careful with our words and deeds as the little ones are following us, waiting for our cue.

The following poem expands on this point.

> There are little eyes upon you, and they are
>   watching night and day;
> There are little ears that quickly take in every
>   word you say;
> There are little hands all eager to do everything
>   you do.
> And a little boy who's dreaming of the day he'll
>   be like you.
>
> You're the little fellow's idol, you're the wisest of
>   the wise,

In his little mind about you, no suspicions ever
    rise;
He believes in you devoutly, holds that all you
    say and do,
He will say and do in your way when he's grown
    up to be like you.

There's a wide-eyed little fellow who believes
    you're always right,
And his ears are always open and he watches day
    and night;
You are setting an example every day in all you do,
For the little boy who's waiting to grow up to be
    like you.
                          —Croft M. Pentz

May all the dads get to realize their responsibility to the little kids who call them "Dad" and who are watching and trying to follow their every move. And may the fathers provide the leadership and influence in their families that have been missing so much in this day and age.

Father Perceptions

Four years—my daddy can do anything!
Seven years—my daddy knows a lot...a whole lot.
Eight years—my father doesn't know quite everything.
Twelve years—oh well, naturally, Father does not know that either.
Fourteen years—oh, Father, he is hopelessly old-fashioned.
Twenty-one years—oh, that man—he is out of date!
Twenty-five years—he knows a little bit about it but not much.
Thirty years—I must find out what Dad thinks about it.
Thirty-five years—before we decide, we'll get Dad's idea first.
Fifty years—what would Dad have thought about that?
Sixty years—my dad knew literally everything.
Sixty-five years—I wish I could talk it over with Dad once more.

FATHERS SHRINK OR expand in size in children's minds depending on what stage of development they may be in. That's just how it is. Children go through these uncertain and unstable situations and this very fact calls for an immoveable rock where children and the family can anchor their lives against the shifting sands of time. And in the end, they will realize how important it was to have a father who didn't flinch, who stayed put and stood firm—a solid anchor for their souls.

And in this regard, it is of utmost importance for the father as the head of the home and priest of the family to have his eyes fixed on "Jesus, the author and finisher of our faith" (Hebrews 12:2).

So now, congratulations fathers! You have your work cut out for you! It's a challenging and difficult one. But don't despair. You have the Holy Spirit guiding and enabling you as you do your God-appointed task.

Faith or Presumption?

A FATHER TOOK his six-year-old boy fishing with him one day. They put out the line and then went up to the cabin. After an hour, they went back down to the river to see if they had caught anything.

Sure enough, there were several fish on the line.

The boy said, "I knew there would be, Daddy."

The father asked, "How did you know?"

"Because I prayed about it," he replied.

So they baited the hooks again and put out the line and went back to the cabin for supper.

Afterward, they went back to the river; again, there were fish on the line.

The boy said, "I knew it."

The father said, "How?"

"I prayed again," said the boy.

So they put the line back into the river and went to the cabin. Before bedtime, they went down again. This time, there were no fish.

The child said, "I knew there wouldn't be."

The father asked, "How did you know?"

The boy said, "Because I didn't pray this time.

The father asked, "And why didn't you pray?"

And the boy said, "Because I remembered that we forgot to bait the hooks."

Our prayer lives can take a lesson from the little boy in our story. We should be honest and sincere in our prayers to God. And when we pray asking for something, let's be sure we are doing what we need to do for our prayers to be answered. Otherwise, it is presumptuous to be asking God for something and perhaps praying for a miracle when we didn't "bait our hooks."

It is called "radical prayer" when we ask the Lord for something and then make ourselves available for God to use to answer our prayer.

Just like when we ask the Lord of the harvest to send laborers to the harvest (Matthew 9:38), we should let him send us among the reapers in answer to our prayer.

Christian Driving

AN HONEST MAN was being tailgated by a stressed-out woman on a busy boulevard. Suddenly, the light turned yellow just in front of him. He did the right thing, stopping at the crosswalk, even though he could have beaten the red light by accelerating through the intersection.

The tailgating woman hit the roof and the horn, screaming in frustration as she missed her chance to get through the intersection with him. As she was still in midrant, she heard a tap on her window and looked up into the face of a very serious police officer. The officer ordered her to exit her car with her hands up. He took her to the police station where she was searched, fingerprinted, photographed, and placed in a cell.

After a couple of hours, a policeman approached the cell and opened the door. She was escorted back to the booking desk where the arresting officer was waiting with her personal effects. He said, "I'm very sorry for this mistake. You see, I pulled up behind your car while you were blowing your horn, flipping the guy off in front of you, and cussing a blue streak at him.

I noticed the "Choose Life" license plate holder, the "What Would Jesus Do?" bumper sticker, the "Follow Me to Sunday School" bumper sticker, and the chrome-plated Christian fish emblem on the trunk. Naturally, I assumed you had stolen the car."

Now, would people recognize that we are Christians by the way we drive?

Designed, Made, and Fixed by the Creator

AN AMERICAN MISSIONARY to the Philippines was vacationing in Baguio, and while there, he took home a souvenir from one of the city's giftshops—a pure silver money clip embellished with a distinctive design. The missionary carried that clip for the next twenty-four years.

One day, it finally broke as he tried to slip a few bills into it. He took the two pieces of the money clip back to the silver shop in Baguio. One workman asked if he could help, and the missionary explained his predicament and laid the pieces into his outstretched hand.

After examining the pieces for a minute or so, he looked up at the missionary and said, "I designed this clip. I was the only one to make this design. I made all of these that were ever made."

"Can you fix it?" the missionary asked.

To which the man replied, "I designed it. I made it. Of course, I can fix it!"

The spiritual application is obvious. Perhaps we feel broken. Our case seems to be hopeless. We fail every time we try to live our lives after Jesus. But as this story so powerfully illustrates the God who designed us and made us has also the power to fix us regardless of the kind of disrepair we are in. All we need to do is go to him. He'll do the rest.

Cleansing Only by the Blood

A LITTLE BOY came running to the house after playing outside. His mother stopped him and asked what was on his right hand.

He replied, "Oh, just a little mud."

His mother then asked if he was planning on getting it off his hand.

He thought for a moment and said, "Sure, Mom. I'll just wipe it off with my other hand."

There was only one problem with the plan: one dirty hand plus one clean hand equals two dirty hands.

Many of us are like that little boy. There may be sin in our lives. But instead of confessing and turning away from it, we try to do something good or praiseworthy. And we somehow think that our good works will cover or outweigh the sins in our lives.

It doesn't work that way. The only solution to the sin problem in our lives can be found in the blood of Jesus Christ, which cleanses us from all of our sins.

St. John says, "But if we walk in the light, as he is in the light, we have fellowship one with another, and the blood of Jesus Christ his Son cleanseth us from all sin" (1 John 1:7).

Let us praise God for sending his Son Jesus to die in our place, and through his blood spilled on the cross, we can have cleansing from all our sins.

Living Up to Your Potential

A STORY IS told of an Indian brave who found an eagle's egg and put it into the nest of a prairie chicken. The eagle hatched with the brood of chicks and grew up with them. All his life, the changeling eagle, thinking he was a prairie chicken, did what the prairie chickens did. He scratched in the dirt for seeds and insects to eat. He clucked and cackled. And he flew in a brief thrashing of wings and flurry of feathers no more than a few feet off the ground. After all, that's how prairie chickens were supposed to fly.

Years passed. And the changeling eagle grew very old. One day, he saw a magnificent bird far above him in the cloudless sky. Hanging with graceful majesty on the powerful wind currents, it soared with scarcely a beat of its strong golden wings.

"What a beautiful bird!" said the changeling eagle to his neighbor. "What is it?"

"That's an eagle, the chief of the birds," the neighbor clucked. "But don't give it a second thought. You could never be like him."

So the changeling never gave it another thought. And it died thinking it was a prairie chicken.

So many of us are like that changeling eagle. We think like the world, talk like the world, act like the world, and even dress like the world. We forget that God has chosen us to be his peculiar people, his holy nation, his royal priesthood to "show forth the praises of him who called us out of darkness into his marvelous light."

Let us not forget that our destination is a place called heaven, and we are getting ready for the society of angelic beings. Let us lift ourselves up from the miasma of our earthly dwelling places and start breathing the pure and unadulterated air of our heavenly home.

Do It Anyway in the Best Way You Know How

HE WAS NOT too well educated, and his manner was somewhat crude and rough, but he became a Christian and was on fire for the Lord. He constantly pestered his pastor to help him be of some genuine service to his church.

In desperation, the pastor gave him a list of ten people saying, "These are members who seldom attend services. Some are prominent men of the city. Contact them any way you can and try to get them to be more faithful. Use the church stationery to write letters if you want but get them back in church."

He accepted the challenge with enthusiasm. About three weeks later, a letter arrived from a prominent physician whose name was on the list. In the envelope was a one thousand dollar check and a note:

> Dear Pastor,
>   Enclosed is my check to make up for my missed offerings. I'm sorry for missing worship so much, but be assured I am going to be present every Sunday from now on and will not by choice miss services again.
>
> Sincerely,
> M. B. Jones, MD

Sometimes, even as we bungle along doing work for the Lord, God takes our best efforts when they are done in the best way we know how and with the purity of motives and sincerity of intentions, and blesses them, for the ultimate praise and glory of his name.

So let's do it. Let not the fear of failure paralyze us in our tracks. Do the good you want to do for the Lord and for his people, and we can be sure he can take care of the rest.

Twenty-Five Beautiful Thoughts

A FRIEND SHARED with me the following beautiful thoughts. They are amusing statements, but they are also so true especially in our spiritual lives and our relationship with God. Here are the following:

1. Give God what's right...not what's left.
2. Man's way leads to hopeless end ... God's way leads to an endless hope.
3. A lot of kneeling will keep you in good standing.
4. He who kneels before God can stand before anyone.
5. In the sentence of life, the devil may be a comma, but never let him be the period.
6. Don't put a question mark where God puts a period.
7. Are you wrinkled with burden? Come to the church for a face-lift.
8. When praying, don't give God instructions...just report for duty.
9. Don't wait for six strong men to take you to church.
10. We don't change God's message... His message changes us.
11. The church is prayer-conditioned.
12. When God ordains, he sustains.
13. Warning: Exposure to the Son may prevent burning.
14. Plan ahead... It wasn't raining when Noah built the ark.
15. Most people want to serve God but only in an advisory position.
16. Suffering from truth decay? Brush up on your Bible.

17. Exercise daily... walk with the Lord.
18. Never give the devil a ride... he will always want to drive.
19. Nothing else ruins the truth like stretching it.
20. Compassion is difficult to give away because it keeps coming back.
21. He who angers you controls you.
22. Worry is the darkroom in which negatives can develop.
23. Give Satan an inch, and he'll be a ruler.
24. Be ye fishers of men... You catch them, and he'll clean them.
25. God doesn't call the qualified; he qualifies the called.

Remember these wonderful thoughts. And by God's grace, live by them because they're just not beautiful thoughts. They are full of wisdom for our spiritual lives.

God Knows What's Best

HAS THERE EVER been a time when you were so disappointed because you didn't get what you want and even blamed God for it? That God doesn't listen to your prayers or that life isn't fair? Only to find in the end that God was saving the best for you.

The following poem bears this truth.

> First, my car broke down
> I was very late for work
> But I missed that awful accident
> Was that your handiwork?
>
> I found a house I loved
> But others got there first
> I was angry, then relieved
> When I heard the pipes had burst!
>
> Yesterday, I found the perfect dress
> But the color was too pale
> Today, I found the dress in red
> Would you believe, it was on sale!
>
> I know you're watching over me
> And I'm feeling truly blessed
> For no matter what I pray for
> You always know what's best!

The scriptures say, "And we know that all things work together for good to those who love God, to those who are the called according to his purpose" (Romans 8:28).

And for this reason, the apostle Paul also says, "Rejoice in the Lord always. Again I will say, rejoice!" (Philippians 4:4).

It is so true. God is all-knowing and so loving he knows what is best, and he'll do what is best for his own.

Lessons from a Trip Down Under 1

WE JUST GOT back from a fun trip to the South Pacific. There were seventy of us, mainly from California with some friends joining us from Nevada, Washington, Oregon, Tennessee, and Canada.

We had quite a few challenges, but the Lord helped us overcome them. First of all, when we got to LAX, we were told that our flight was cancelled because our plane that was doing some ground maneuvers hit a loader that was not working and not parked properly, damaging the plane's wing. The staff of Qantas Airways were able to book all of us on a later flight to Sydney, Australia, via Brisbane. Nine of us, however, had to take a domestic flight from Brisbane to Sydney. And although they came many hours later, they too were given a tour of the city and finally joined us at the hotel later that night.

Another unfortunate incident that occurred happened to Danny Dizon. We were concluding our tour of New Zealand when he had a mild stroke that affected his sense of balance and slurred his speech. We took him to the hospital where he was fully examined and treated. By God's grace, he was discharged two days later and was able to fly back home with wife, Merlinda, so he could get full and better treatment here. He is now home, and with our continuing prayers, he is hoping for a speedy and full recovery.

We live in a sinful and imperfect world, and things happen beyond our control that dash our hopes and mar our happiness. But God is still in control. He can say to the enemy and the elements,

"Thus far and no farther!" And his will is obeyed. One day soon, we will be in a perfect world. And there will be perfect peace, happiness, and safety forevermore.

Lessons from a Trip Down Under 2

THE SOUTH PACIFIC is a different world. It was summertime when our plane left Los Angeles International Airport, and when it taxied down the runway at the Sydney International Airport, it was in the dead of winter. We were relieved to be away from the oppressive heat that was punishing the States. And here we were on tour in Australia with our layered clothing and heavy jackets, mufflers, mittens, and all.

The Blue Mountains were awesome—blue because of a bluish haze that lifted from the valley floor as sunlight struck the gum trees down below. It was a spectacular sight, and one might call this place the Grand Canyon of the South Pacific. The people there, however, pride themselves in saying that while there was a time that the Grand Canyon of the United States was only about two inches deep, the Blue Mountains were cavernously deep from the beginning of time.

We took a train that brought us straight down the steepest and most incline railway in the world! Then a fifteen-minute boardwalk through a jungle of towering trees and greenery led us to where we could board the skyway lift, flying us back across dizzying heights to our station. It was an exhilarating and unique experience, not to mention the rare sight of flocks of white cockatoos frolicking among the branches of the wild.

It was also great watching kangaroos walking around with their little ones safely tucked in their pouches and koalas munching on the leaves of eucalyptus trees. We saw emus, penguins, and other wildlife unique only in that part of the world.

As we were driving around Sydney taking in the sights and sounds of the city, our guide pointed us to a government building that displayed the official seal of New South Wales. It had both the images of the kangaroo and the emu on it. He then remarked that the people chose to have these images on their seal because among the animals of the wild, these two were the only ones that couldn't move backward. This was a constant reminder to the people that the only move they should make as a nation is a move forward.

I thought this was an interesting point. And how great it would be if in our Christian walk we were like the kangaroo and the emu—unable to move backward that when we moved, the only direction we would go is forward. This is possible when we run the race of our spiritual life with patience...looking unto Jesus the author and finisher of our faith.

Lessons from a Trip Down Under 3

SYDNEY AND MELBOURNE are rival cities in many ways. In terms of natural beauty and tourist attractions, Sydney may have the edge with its beautiful harbor and scenic waterways. Melbourne, however, is the site of major competitions in sports not only for Australia but for the South Pacific although both cities hosted the world Olympic games (Sydney in 2000 and Melbourne in 1956). Melbourne also takes pride in its history. They like to remind the Sydney inhabitants that their ancestors came to settle in Sydney in chains and against their will while Melbourne was founded by people who came on their own free will. And the comparison and contrast go on.

The Sunday we were in Melbourne, we had the morning free. Some of us decided to get on the train and explore the countryside. Others took the city tram to enjoy more of the city sights and landmarks. A few others went shopping.

But for a few of us, we had a wonderful surprise. Our youngest daughter, Jane, who was with us on this trip was reading about the tourist sites of the city and learned that some of the indoor and outdoor tennis courts of the Rod Laver Arena were available to the public for a fee. Now this was something special. I have been to Wimbledon and Roland Garros and watched the games there. But to be able to play in Melbourne, where the first Grand Slam Tennis Tournament of the year is held, was exciting. So I bought a pair of tennis shoes, rented a racket, picked up some balls, and took to the courts. We were ecstatic, never mind that our audience was just a few friends cheering us on the sidelines. For us, this was going to be an experience we will all long remember.

Our tour that evening was going to be another unforgettable one. Our guide took us on a two-hour drive to Phillip's Island where we were going to watch a unique phenomenon of nature and a world-class tourist attraction called "The Penguin Parade." We walked down a short distance to the beach and made ourselves comfortable on the bleachers. Night was falling, and the ocean breeze was getting chilly. We sat there quietly in anticipation of these little creatures of the sea.

Not too long after dusk, the first of the penguins began coming out of the sea onto the land. We noticed how they came to land in groups of ten to fifteen. We particularly observed that only one or two would come out of the water first, walking a few steps and look-ing around, obviously checking to see if there were any predatory creatures or dangerous animals around. Then the lead penguin goes back to the water, and in a few seconds, the whole group gets on the land and head to their burrows. This would be the end of the day for these fairy penguins who have gone out to sea early in the morning and searched for food all day in the water.

Penguins are tiny creatures of the sea, but we can learn valuable lessons from them. They are known to be loyal to their mates and are protective of their young. They also care very much about each other. And as we have observed, they move around in groups, making sure of the safety of everyone.

Hey, how about caring for each other and looking out for each other's safety as penguins do? We should see more of this among brothers and sisters in the family of God.

Lessons from a Trip Down Under 4

New Zealand is a land of beauty and wonder. The green hills and verdant meadows dotted with herds of cattle and flocks of sheep are a delight to the eye and relaxing to the mind. There are spectacular geysers, sulfur hot springs and lakes.

Golf, though not as popular as rugby in terms of a national pastime, is played there pretty much. As a matter of fact, some of the golf courses in the country are listed among the top one hundred golf courses in the world. So no surprise that some of us managed to get a foursome together in Auckland and went to play in a nearby golf course. The group included Dr. Felcar Morada, Pat Bascon, Albert Bagingito, and myself. It didn't matter that it rained part of the time. We just had to seek shelter under the trees when it poured. It only added excitement to what would become a memorable experience for us.

We were also treated to a number of performances featuring the fascinating culture of the Maori people. We participated in their rituals like the rubbing of the noses between the leaders of the visitor group and the local tribe following the ceremony of the "Welcome Leaf."

And we sat down to watch their warriors as they danced with frenzy to the sound of drums and gongs with their eyeball—popping and tongue—extending routines that were meant to drive the evil spirits away.

The kiwi, a flightless nocturnal bird that is becoming an endangered species and the silver fern are New Zealand's national symbols.

But the sheep could have served as well, considering that the nation prides itself with the abundance of its wool. We were at the Agrodome in Rotorua, and as many as eighteen breeds of sheep performed for us. I didn't know sheep could be actors too! A sheep-shearing demonstration was also done that gave more meaning to the prophet Isaiah's words as applied to Jesus, "As a sheep before its shearers is dumb" (Isaiah 53:7).

The glow worm caves, however, were probably the most enchanting. The multichambered caverns teemed with beautiful stalactite and stalagmite formations. While riding on small boats and navigating the water underground, we looked up and on the roof of the caves just above our heads, the glow worms were perched, shining in the dark like stars and constellations on a moonless night.

Every now and then, I think of those glow worms. I know that in the bosom of the earth, in some dark caves in New Zealand, the glow worms continue to shine in the darkness, regardless of what's going on in the world above them. And I want to be like a glow worm—with my light shining amid the darkness regardless of what may be going on in the world around me. Wouldn't you?

Jesus said, "Let your light so shine before men that they may see your good works; and glorify your Father which is in heaven" (Matthew 5:16).

Lessons from a Trip to the Fiji Islands

THE FIJI ISLANDS are an entirely different world. It was also winter season there, but it was a delightsome eighty-two degrees compared to the chilling fifty-five degrees temperatures of Australia and New Zealand.

So having packed away the mittens, mufflers, and heavy clothes, we donned our hats, shades, sunblock lotion, shorts, and other beach stuff. There was plenty of sun, sand, and water, and we were ready to soak everything in.

We first visited an authentic Fiji village where we received a warm traditional Fijian hospitality after participating in their welcoming rites. Then we did an island cruise where we were treated to nonstop entertainment by the crew as the boat split the crystal-clear blue waters of the ocean.

Island activities for the day included swimming, kayaking, and snorkeling in a vast and colorful coral strand and just lying down lazily on the white sand in a shady nook of the island. The noon meal was superb. And we partook of the lavish delicacies to our hearts' desire.

We had a few more memorable experiences like our visit to the caves where we saw cannibal ovens that were in use in some distant past, going down the river on a bamboo raft, and swimming in the warm waters as we moved along, getting entertained in many ways through their song and dance and other cultural presentations, and of course, enjoying the pineapples, young coconuts, and sweet papayas as much as we could.

But the most impressive sight for me to behold was that of one of our group members Violeta Bagingito in a wheelchair atop the platform of a canoe that ferried passengers from the big boat to our picnic island and pleasure cove for the day. Here was this Glendale, California, resident who in the face of so many odds, braved flying thousands of miles through the air, over land and sea, to be able to set foot on the white sand beaches of these exotic islands of the South Pacific. The scene spoke volumes to me. It spoke of a dream realized, of dogged determination, of patience and long-suffering, and ultimately of an undying devotion and steadfast loyalty particularly of a husband to his wife.

I was so happy for them and actually was so excited about this whole experience at that special moment in time. And I wondered, if it was me in that situation, would I have been able to do it? And if it was you, would you have been able to do the same?

Giving Thanks for All Things

SCOTTISH MINISTER ALEXANDER Whyte was known for his uplifting prayers in the pulpit. He always found something for which to be grateful. One morning, the weather was so gloomy that a church member thought to himself, "Certainly the preacher won't think of anything for which to thank the Lord on a wretched day like this." Much to his surprise, however, Whyte began by praying, "We thank Thee, O God, that it is not always like this."

That's why the apostle Paul could say, "Giving thanks always for all things unto God and the Father in the name of our Lord Jesus Christ" (Ephesians 5:20). Because although there is so much evil and trouble in the world around us, if we look closely, there will always be some bright spot we can be grateful for. And when we open up our hearts in gratitude to God, he gives us more reason to rejoice.

Our gratitude is not based on circumstances. It's not the weather, nor is it our material prosperity or even our personal health. In an evanescent and shifting world, nothing is permanent (only death and taxes!). Everything is changing and as permanent as shifting sand. What we need is a stable and rock-like basis for our gratitude and joy.

The prophet Habakkuk says,

> Although the fig tree shall not blossom, neither
> [shall] fruit [be] in the vines;
> the labour of the olive shall fail, and the fields shall
> yield no meat; the flock shall be cut off from the
> fold, and [there shall be] no herd in the stalls:

Yet I will rejoice in the LORD, I will joy in the
God of my salvation.
—Habakkuk 3:17–18

This explains why even when our circumstances change for the worse, we can continue to be grateful because the reason for our gratitude is not our fickle and changing circumstances but the unfailing love of God. We will be forever and continually grateful due to the saving act of God and his mercy toward us in the sacrificial death of our Lord and Savior Jesus Christ.

So let's be thankful, everyone. Let this mind-set be ours every day of every year of our lives.

About the Author

SIMEON P. ROSETE Jr. was born in the Philippines and earned a degree in the history and philosophy of religion at Philippine Union College, now Adventist University of the Philippines. He went on to do his master's degree in theology and public health at the Seventh-day Adventist Theological Seminary (Far East) in Manila, Philippines. He would later earn the degree of doctor of biblical studies at the Master's International School of Divinity at Evansville, Indiana.

He served as a pastor, department director, and finally, president of the Mountain Provinces Mission of Seventh-day Adventists with headquarters at Baguio City, Philippines. He was elected president at the age of twenty-eight, making him the youngest Mission president in the history of the work of the Seventh-day Adventist Church in the Philippines.

He was called to serve as the senior pastor of the Central Filipino Seventh-day Adventist Church at Los Angeles, California, a six-hundred-member congregation and the first Filipino Seventh-day Adventist Church established in the United States and Canada. He has served this congregation for twenty-five years now and was instrumental in the construction of its sanctuary and gymnasium complex. In between his ministry to the Central Filipino Church, he served as director of the Asian Pacific Region of the Southern California Conference of Seventh-day Adventists with headquarters at Glendale, California, and also served as senior pastor of the Glendale Filipino Seventh-day Adventist Church, Glendale, California.

He is married to the former Ellen Pacheco with whom he has four children and four grandkids.

CPSIA information can be obtained
at www.ICGtesting.com
Printed in the USA
FSHW010728110719